FIGMENTS
Parts of imagination

AND

FRAGMENTS
Parts of remembrance

Edited by Jim Powers

Illustrated by Frank Boros

Book Layout by Maritza Mcmillan

ISBN: 978-0-615-36988-4

Library of Congress Control Number: 2010905954

Printed in the United States of America

Fables for adults, perhaps. Stories that might conjure images. Stories of fun and thought. What are we but stories, part figment, part fragment of imaginations.

Richard Everett Upton

FOR MY FRIENDS

CONTENTS

THE FERRYBOAT

For Whitney
you are wonderful!

Richard Everett Upton

WE lived on Barrow Street in 1934. Barrow Street is in Greenwich Village. Our house was number 97, which was between Hudson Street and Greenwich Street. Next door was a large factory building that runs between Barrow Street and Morton Street, as I remember it, facing Greenwich Street. The Ninth Avenue El ran up Greenwich Street to Fourteenth Street, where it became Ninth Avenue. Across the street was a compound of buildings belonging to St. Luke's Chapel. St. Luke's was a chapel because it belonged to Trinity Parish. Trinity Church on Broadway at Wall Street is one of the most famous landmarks of New York City.

The block On Hudson Street bound by Barrow Street and Christopher Street to Greenwich Street was all St. Luke's. The church still stands on Hudson Street mid-block surrounded by its outcrop of buildings. It was then as it is now, a neighborhood.

One Sunday morning I ventured into St. Luke's in the middle of the nine-thirty or children's mass. There was a buxom lady there who seemed to be in charge. She took me by the hand and led me up to the front of the church. Not a word was spoken. It was as if I was expected. I didn't know what to do. I was 'roaming' and thought to poke my head in the door and look around. Little did I know what was going on, but, there I was being led by the hand by this in charge woman to the front of the church. I didn't protest. I knew that there would be a chance to escape sometime I didn't speak: because when she bent over me and put her finger to her lips as if to shush me.

After the service, where I had observed what everyone else was doing, including crossing myself and genuflecting and singing hymns as the rest of the children did, we went across the courtyard to the parish house for cocoa and buns. There were people who spoke to me then. The Priest asked my name and where I lived. I told him. And before I knew it I was in Sunday school.

I went home later, and my parents were as usual, frantic. I told them what I had done, and they seemed pleased. My roams were not new to them, but they were concerned never the less. Later that week the Priest came to visit my mother, and from then on I went to church on Sunday, and Wednesday afternoons after school. Eventually I became and Episcopalian. My mother and father never tired of telling people how I chose my religion all by myself. I think, truth to be told, I had never thought about it for a moment, I was sucked into the church by a domineering buxom woman.

I was seven years old and went to private school. City and Country School had been founded by Caroline Pratt and was a progressive school. Its curriculum was unorthodox so far as learning institutions went, but in the long run provided very good education. Its graduates went on to 'good schools'. It was located on Eleventh Street and ran through to Twelfth Street between Sixth and Seventh Avenues.

I walked to school every day. Anyone who knows the 'Village' will tell you that is quite a hike for a lad of seven. I never thought about it, and obviously, my parents were not terribly worried. The world was a safer for children.

The Christopher Street Ferry ran at the end of Christopher Street to Hoboken Terminal where, I believe, the Erie-Lackawanna railroad terminated. It and other railroads terminated their runs in New Jersey because New York Central and Pennsylvania railroads had a monopoly on Stations in Manhattan.

In those days, there were a lot of ferry boats running between New Jersey and Manhattan. You could ride all the way from the Battery to One Hundred and Twenty Fifth Street on ferryboats. Some mornings I would wake early and steal a nickel from my mother and run down to the ferryboat dock and ride the boat across the River and I would stay on the boat and ride back. One day one of the crew told me that when I got to Hoboken to run up to the next slip and ride the boat to Twenty Third Street, and back, which I did, it was quite an adventure except when I returned my parents were up and frantic.

One time I was able to go from Christopher Street all the way to the Fifty-Seventh Street pier. Cross-town busses met the ferryboats from New Jersey, and took their passengers across town to the East River. So it was really a shuttle service. The ferries met the boats at important cross-town junctures, although I don't remember a Thirty-Fourth Street ferry. There may have been. The day I really took my 'sea adventure' was the day I got on at Christopher Street and spent a whole voyage going from shore to shore to shore until I had done the whole thing. It had to be a Saturday. That was the only day I would have had that kind of time to spend sailing the seas of the Hudson River.

The fantasy you conjure when you look down into the waters flowing fast beneath the boat. You arrive at the other side of the great water. The mighty ship eases into its slip nudging the flexible sides until she is secure at the dock. The mighty deck hands pull chains to make the ship even with the pier.

The gates open, trucks and cars rumble off the boat. People rush toward 'customs officers' at the Lackawanna railroad who directed them to waiting trains. It was pretty heady stuff for a seven year old. I ran to the gates that would open for the next voyage and made myself scarce until the mighty ship boarded its waiting throng headed for the other side of the mighty sea.

The whistle sounded; once again, we headed out to unknown uncharted waters where all the danger you could imagine waited. The boat might sink, or worse, an enemy boat attack and take us as prisoners of war. So many things could happen between here and there. When we got safely to the other side, I changed boats; I was going to South America to explore the mighty Amazon. South America was part of what we were learning about in school.

If I had another nickel, I bought a hot dog with mustard and Sauerkraut. It was first class dining. I have had a life long passion for grilled hotdogs, and am somewhat a connoisseur of them. There was nothing like a Nedicks hot dog and an orange drink. The whole thing cost a dime. And, that, at the time was lunch for many people. Actually Nedicks was a wonderful place. You could have breakfast; an orange drink, a doughnut, and a cup of coffee for a dime. The hot dog by itself cost a nickel.

On the corner of Greenwich Avenue and Christopher Street there was a diner that had a sign in the window; Blueberry Pie Ala Mode, fifteen cents. I used to crave it every time I walked by, I didn't now what it was, but I wanted some.

I could ride all day long on the Subway for a nickel. I never got off and went through the turnstile, because it meant I had to sneak back in, and that was fun. I waited just outside the turnstile until the train came into the station, then I ducked under the stile and ran for the train before the doors closed. Sometimes the man in the change booth would yell after me, it was part of the fun. I got on, and if I were with a friend, we would laugh hysterically at what we had done.

This was the beginning of a youthful life and time of roaming.
After a while, my parents got used to the idea I was safe roaming the streets of New York. I always seemed to know where I was going. I don't think they were pleased with the idea as a whole, but thought I probably was in no danger. After all, I managed to walk to school and back. When you have no fear, you plow ahead.

I got there most mornings by nine, but some mornings I dawdled along and got there late, usually because I had stops to make. Sutter's bakery was on Bleeker Street and one of the ways I went to school. I'd stop and smell the wonderful aroma coming from the shop as they baked wonderful things to tempt anyone passing by. I would stop and with my nose plastered to it, look in the window. Mr. Sutter knew who I was and would sometimes give me a cookie, then when my mother came in tell her. My mother would feign horror at my begging and scold me, and Mr. Sutter would give me another cookie.

There was a flower shop where I would stop and smell the flowers. The shop owner knew me because I would look longingly at the flowers wanting all of them. Once in a while he gave me one to take to my teacher because I was late. I loved school, but hated going there. Life was much more interesting outside of school.

Some years later, when I didn't go to private school, but to PS forty-one on Greenwich Avenue, I played hooky for several days. I think, at that time I was riding on a tug boat, or doing something adventurous. My mother was called to school by Mrs. Chisholm, who was the principal. Mrs. Chisholm was a buxom woman, as large in front, as she was in the rear. She was imposing to say the least. I went to school with George Orteig. His family owned the Lafayette Hotel in Greenwich Village. George's grandfather is the man who rewarded Mr. Lindberg with twenty-five thousand Dollars for flying solo across the Atlantic. The Orteig family sent Mrs. Chisholm a spray of orchids for every occasion when there was an assembly, like graduation. Mrs. Chisholm wore them and looked like a racehorse after winning a stakes race.

Mrs. Chisholm summoned my mother to her presence. My mother was a tiny woman, four feet eleven, with a gorgeous figure. Her clothes in her youth had been made by Worth in Paris, and she still had them. This day she wore a Worth suit of blue tweed, silk blouse, white gloves and navy blue shoes and a smart Parisian hat. She was tiny. She sat in her chair sideways because if she had sat in it straight back her legs would be off the floor. Mrs. Chisholm walked in front of my mother and told her my playing hooky was a very serious business. My mother sat very calmly while Mrs. Chisholm explained playing hooky was against the law. Finally she stopped. As I remember the day, Mrs. Chisholm wore a patterned dress with a large white collar. With her grey hair tightly curled alamode, she still looked like a racehorse. She wore nose glasses, which shook when she talked. They waggled the more animated she got. She adjusted them and continuing talking.

My mother sat and listened, and said nothing. Mrs. Chisholm paused expecting, I am sure, a deep apology for my behavior. My mother stood and faced her and said, to the effect; "Well, Mrs. Chisholm, if you made school an interesting place for Richard to be, perhaps he wouldn't be inclined to play hooky".

Later I returned to my class. Teachers in those days taught all subjects in one room. I was in the fourth grade. My teacher was Mrs. McLester. She was a wiry woman, I would guess, in her fifties with red hair. Whether or not it was her red hair we didn't know. Every morning when we came into class, you could smell liquor on her. She would send the 'Chinese boy' down to the candy store to get her 'a cuppa cawfee an' a bananer'. She would drink the coffee as she taught first period. She would have the banana for lunch. I told my Godmother Mrs. McLester always smelled of liquor. My Godmother said; "I don't blame her, if I had to teach all you little bastards I would be drunk too". I returned to class. Mrs. Mc Lester was in rare form.

She came over to me and pointed her bony finger at me and said; "Yer on the hook! Yr goin' t'refoum school, that's what, yr on the way to refoum school". I sat at my desk and wondered what she was talking about, what is reform school? I was not an easy child.

When I was seven and went to City and Country School My parents were in the throes of divorce. At the last minute, my mother couldn't sign the necessary papers to give me to my Godparents as an adopted son. Her reneging changed the course of my life. I had, for months lived with my Godparents as their 'son'. It never occurred to me I was to 'be' their son in fact. My parents were not on my mind. At the time, they were removed from me emotionally. I never thought of them as my 'parents'. It was complicated in that, I had never thought of my mother and father as 'my parents'. I honestly didn't know what 'parents' were. They were my 'mother and father' and I didn't understand what that meant. My life had been a nomadic sort of thing, in that my mother and father spent very little time together. My God parents became my parents; my 'loyalties' were to them.

My parents decided not to divorce, dammit! It was a time of 'fashionable psychology', which was somewhat new, and it dictated I should begin to build a life with my parents. My thinking, quite clearly, was this was not what I wanted at all. My life with my godparents was somewhat luxurious. My life with my parents at the moment was catch can. I was not a pleased boy. My real parents were interlopers in my life. It was not that they were not nice people;

it was just they were not 'my kind' of people. I moved with them to Ninety Seven Barrow Street and continued to go to City and Country School. The tuition was paid. It was at this juncture I decided adventure was the one thing I wanted; hence the ferry boat rides at the crack of dawn. My fantasy was about running away on a ship. In those days, ships sailed into New York Harbor as often as planes land at Kennedy. They came from all over the world. Their cargos smelled of spices and herbs. It was very exotic. The waterfront was totally different than it is today, so different it is hard to describe. The West Side Highway was built so automobile traffic could move up and down the west side of New York. Twelfth Avenue was the waterfront. From the battery to Fifty Ninth Street was one pier after another with ships sailing into their berths every day. It was a very busy harbor. The New Jersey side of the Hudson had nearly as many piers as the Manhattan side of the Hudson. There was no end to traffic on the river.

Great ships would sail up the river to the passenger piers, silent giants attended by tugboats tooting at each other. Once in awhile the Leviathan would trumpet back, and continue her silent way toward her berth above forty second street. There was a ship docked on the New Jersey side of the Hudson named 'Leviathan' It was a ship that was doomed with bad luck and sat for years across the Hudson silent and alone. It was done in for scrap and sold to Japan to be used for war materiel in the Second World War.

The great liners were referred to as 'leviathans' for their great size and beauty. And the great ships were beautiful; they looked like 'ships'. Today they look like floating giant hotels. This is not a bad thing in itself; it is what I remember ships looked like.

On the street where the docks met the city, West Street, or Twelfth Avenue there was pandemonium on a pier when a great ship docked. This was nearly every day. Cabs and limousines waited and people rushed into the bowels of the pier to meet disembarking passengers. Then the wait began. There was customs to wade through. First Class Passengers were served first. Trunks were opened and contents displayed. Slowly the passengers made their way to waiting family

and friends. Porters with trucks loaded the baggage high, and owners followed dutifully behind with their greeters. Some passengers had dogs on leashes who barked happily being on firm ground again some were a little shaky with their 'sea legs'.
Limousines waited on the loading dock. Many times there were two, one for the passengers, and one for the luggage and perhaps a maid who traveled with her mistress. In all, it was gala.

Ship travel was the only way to get to Europe, or any other place on earth, at that time. Flying was new and the most you could fly was from city to close by city. Ship Travel allowed you to take a very large wardrobe with you. Going abroad and staying was considered to be a usual event.

Transcontinental train travel was the other destination carrier. You could travel anywhere in the United States by train. Tracks crisscrossed the nation East and West, North and South. You could go first class in a compartment or Pullman, upper or lower berth, or in the coaches. Just like flying is today. The one exception was the dining car and the observation car. They were open for everyone's use. You could have the same meal if you sat in a coach seat as the millionaire who traveled in a compartment. It was democratic; the only difference was the fare you paid.

You could travel by bus. Busses sometimes took days to get to their destinations, but it was cheap, the stops frequent, and sometimes people stayed in a city or town for a night just to get into a bed. It was cramped traveling at best. We went once to Denver by bus, I thought it was fun. It was at a nadir in our lives.

Other times when my mother took us to Denver to visit my grandparents we took the Twentieth Century Limited. Depending on family finances at the time decided whether we were in a Pullman berth or in a compartment. We changed in Chicago to the Denver Zephyr. It was a new streamline train all shiny and silver.

There were always several hours to wait between trains, so we went into Chicago itself and had lunch or sight saw. Once we went to the convent where my Great Aunt had been a Nun. She had been a painter and painted a portrait of Pope Pius Tenth.

I loved travel, loved getting ready and boarding and the trip. I hated arriving. It meant the end to the trip. I especially disliked arriving home. It meant life picked itself up and continued, usually to school. My idea of heaven was to be able to get off a train and onto a boat that would take me to exotic 'ports of call'. The movies were full of exotic ports of call. Hedy Lamar was usually the siren luring unsuspecting leading men astray, but always in Tangier or Macao, or some other Geography book locale.

My world was the exploration of New York or Denver or Boston for the most part, and not Denver or Boston, too much. Supervision was strict and running around was not looked upon with great favor. However, New York was another story.

I had freedom.

New York was a compact city in that it had everything in abundance. Here nothing lacked for adventure. No matter where you were, you would come into something new. Other cities have small downtown sections where all the hustle and bustle was, perhaps a few blocks. Then the city would fan itself out into neighborhoods. New York was a tall building city. They were and are, more than ever today, a city of tall buildings. It is amazing to think that one office building holds the number of people to populate a small city, that one district has enough tall buildings to comprise a city of medium size. One block in midtown Manhattan is the entire down town part of some cities. I looked at Manhattan in those days and found my oyster; that was the pearl of my adventure.

Of course, today it has doubled in size, but in the thirties and forties, it was still quite a tall city. As a child I was in awe of elevators in office buildings. They were manned by men with white gloves who snapped those elevators into action when they were sent aloft by the starters. 'All spit and polish'. The Army had nothing on these Men. A trip to the top of The Empire State Building was so exciting; the elevators hummed their way into the sky to the eighty-eighth floor where you transferred to elevators to the tower observation platform.

It was pure adrenalin, a great high. Then you went outside. You would never go to the Empire State Building on a cloudy or rainy day, so the weather was spectacular. The view captured miles and miles of your vision in all directions, to the hills of Montclair New Jersey in the West, east to the Atlantic then to Long Island City to Long Island Sound and Connecticut shore, north to the hills of Westchester County. All clear as a bell.

If I looked down, I got a tightened feeling in my testicles at the thought of falling so many floors. They said that when a person jumped from the observation platform, they died on the way down from speed and loss of air. It didn't seem to me it was true. In my head it was a 'splat' on the sidewalk. I mean, to me, if you made the choice to jump, that was it, no second thoughts there. There were no barriers to prevent them who would take the plunge stop and reconsider. Today there are barriers that discourage anyone from trying.

Actually, a few years before, so they say, many jumped from office building windows at the time of the crash! So height made no difference if that was your way of getting to the bottom fast. I guess it was more glamorous jumping from the Empire State Building, more like a lovelorn thing, or life isn't all its cracked up to be. People's biography's offer only highlights to a persons' life. They obviously can't recount those hours and days in between descriptive sentences of their lives. How can a few hundred pages describe years of living. And, do you ever really get to know the person ascribed? You get thumb nail impressions, anecdotes, and events, but few of the terrors most lives hold. So it is now, I describe a New York I remember, and it is an impression. Things do stand out.

The Normandie was to sail up the Hudson River on her Maiden Voyage, one day I believe in July. I suppose it is historically recorded what day it was, in any case, it was an event. At the foot of Morton

Street was a recreational pier. It was a wrought iron super structure, probably late Eighteen Eighty's. It was a place where people literally camped out on hot summer nights. By day, it was a pier where children played games and old women and men sat in the breeze reading Italian News Papers, or whatever paper they read.
The Normandie was the largest and fastest passenger ship to travel from Europe to the United States. It was the largest and the fastest in the world. The next year it was bumped by the Queen Mary being larger and nominally faster. This was Normandie's day. It was a beautiful summer day, and there was a crowd of people. A band was assembled and played for the crowd; probably the same one that gave concerts on Sunday afternoons.

We stood waiting for the ship to majestically make her way up the Hudson. When you wait in anticipation for something, it takes forever to get there. And it seemed like it did. However, in the distance we heard horns and whistles of tug boats and fireboats, and sure enough, in the distance we saw this behemoth gliding up the river. Now and then, we heard a deep booming of its foghorn.

Then it was upon us. It seemed close enough to touch the pier. Of course it wasn't, but people screamed in terror at its size and shrank away from the railing of the pier. The foghorn blasted just as it passed the pier. The pier shuddered from the vibration. We all yelled and screamed at the boat, welcoming it to New York. It must have heard us because it boomed again. As I remember, one woman fainted and several people peed their pants.

I had a Dowager Aunt traveling to France, and she was proud to be going on the Maiden Voyage back to France. She traveled First Class, naturally. Now, as part of my investigation of things, I had gone up to the French Line, and by a stroke of luck, met someone who was not in charge, but had the ability to get me on board to see the ship. It was a wonderland. Ships have always held me in thrall, but this was more than I could imagine in my wildest dreams. I became the 'darling' of the ship personnel. Nothing would do but that I had to see everything, and I saw as much as I could.

When I went home, it was late; my parent's sangfroid was not a whole lot more than 'froid'. When I told them where I had been, of course, they didn't believe me.

I was almost forbidden to see my Aunt off on her journey. But they couldn't cheat me out of the thrill of getting on the Normandie. So off we went to the French Line. My parents dressed me in hand me downs; short pants knee socks and jacket. In those days even the richest handed `down. My cousins were all shopped for at Saks, Lord and Taylor and Best and Co. and other great department stores. So I scrubbed up well.

My Aunt had arrived from the Plaza by car, with her maid, earlier, so she was ensconced in her suite. The Maid was unpacking. As we boarded the ship one of the crew smiled and said "Richard, nice to see you again, are you sailing with us today?" I told him I wasn't, but that my Aunt was. My parents were somewhat bemused by this. As we made our way up to my Aunt's suite in First Class, more and more of the crew I'd met remembered me. We chatted like old friends; I introduced them to my parents. I was, perhaps nine. My parents were not only bemused, they were in shock. I had told the truth.

When we arrived at my Aunt's suite we were ushered in to the 'drawing room' or salon, by her maid. Other people were there, some of my cousins were in New York, so they were there. The suite was full of flowers and Champagne flowed. A waiter came in bringing hors d'oeuvres, and he said hello to Richard too. This caused no end of consternation among my cousins who were far better traveled than me, and were very snooty to boot. They wanted to know how it was I knew a waiter on the Normandie. I told them I had been on the ship and had a grand tour, and even met the captain. They didn't believe me, so I told them I would show them around. Which I did. There were several more 'hellos' from the people I'd met which put their noses out of joint for sure.

Then came the coup, walking down the corridor on the upper deck was the Captain of the Normandie. He smiled, and said 'hello'. My cousins were waiting. Then he stopped, and said, "Aren't you the little boy I met before?" I told him yes, he said, "You are Richard?" I nodded, "Ah, yes, how nice to see you again, are you sailing with us today?" I told him no, but that my aunt was, and told him who she was. He smiled and said "Merci, I shall remember" and he did; she sat at the Captain's table. She never really forgave me for upstaging her. I am sure she enjoyed the Captain's table.

When we returned to my Aunt's suite, my cousins told her what they knew. She was furious someone had dared to be aboard the Normandie before her, and knew the crew. Not only had that but met the captain too. Her idea of travel was to associate only with those people who were worthy of her presence. If their forefathers came to America after 1700 they were obviously not worth the attention, unless of course you were a Vanderbilt or Astor. The Astors were on shaky ground, after all they were fur traders, and Jewish, but rich, which seemed to give them cache. Boston's grand dames were not terribly democratic, socially.

After this incident, my parents were not too restrictive regarding my travels abroad. They didn't question when I brought home salami from the Rex, or Bratwurst from the Bremen. The crew on the ships must have thought I was a cute street urchin snuck aboard for food. It was the depression. Undoubtedly, dressed in my overalls and shirt I must have looked like countless thousands of New York children, scruffy and 'poor'. In any case I brought home many things from the ships, and my parents were always in wonderment with my prizes.

In those days, many children were put out of their homes by parents who could not afford to keep them. These were children ranging in age nine up to thirteen or fourteen. They traveled all over the country looking for homes, or just surviving. The phrase 'write when you get work' was no joke, why waste a three-cent stamp if you weren't working. If you were working, send money.

I wasn't poor or unfed. It was my fascination with ships. To me they represented freedom into the unknown; adventure waited on board each of them. They were majestic, even to the smallest of them. I remember a cousin sailed on the Samaria, a 29,000 tonner of the

White Star Line, later Cunard. She was a dowdy little ship built before world war one, a one stacker. A friend and I were to sail on her from Canada in 1951, we had a one-way passage, how we planned to return was never thought of, it was an adventure. We never did sail on her, but the thrill of possibility endured.

The next year saw the arrival of the Queen Mary; it was much the same scene at the recreation pier. When her majesty of the seas hoved into sight, it was just as thrilling. Indeed she was enormous, but she had little style while the Normandie was sleek and modem. Nor did I fare as well on the Queen Mary as I did the Normandie. She was an English ship, and there was very little room for little boys to explore all there was. That year no one was making the maiden voyage to Southampton. I did go on when she sailed, as one of many thousands who boarded her, seeing passengers off. I blended in with a group going aboard; I had my ticket, and presented it as a boy grown up with his own ticket.

Once aboard I was unfettered to roam as I wished. I peeked into staterooms over flowing with people, who smiled, and must have thought I belonged to another stateroom. I happened to be on the promenade deck when the first of the three warning horns sounded to get visitors ashore. The noise almost threw me into the river.   I clung to the rail in terror.   I had only heard a noise like this from a distance. It was the fog horn.   Now it was right there, BOOOOOOOOOOOOOOOOOM! When it stopped, my ears rang like church bells. I literally ran into the ship. With my ears still ringing, I saw the first class lounge and dining salon, people had already begun to line up for seating.

The second horn sounded, and even in the ship, it shuddered through making everything rustle a bit. It was time to begin seriously thinking about getting off the ship. Crew members were saying "all ashore who are going ashore, all ashore who are going ashore"

Stewards in crisp uniforms were ringing chimes and the air was filled with electric anticipation, for them who sailed and for them who were seeing them off, champagne glasses were raised a last time, kisses flowed like wine, corsages were in evidence every where. I watched the multitude go down the gangplank from every class.

The ship's horn boomed the last time. The gangplanks were being readied to be hauled in. I wondered what would happen to a 'little boy' who stowed away. It was the temptation of a lifetime. Should I do it? Quickly the options flew through my mind. I could hide. I could pretend to belong to someone else; there were a myriad of options. I could also be put off onto the pilot boat, which would cost my parents about fifty dollars, which they wouldn't appreciate.

At the very last moment I ran for the gang plank and just made it crashing into the arms of a man at the end of the gangplank.

Then I ran to the end of the pier and watched as the great ship slide from her berth amid 'tootings' from her tugboats, and short blasts from her foghorn which was not nearly so daunting as it was on the top deck of the ship, but it was enough to impress me.

It would be fifty plus years before I ever sailed on an ocean liner. It was on the Vista Fjord, a trip from Kiel to Genoa. That is another story.

I had many adventures, but the glamour of the Queens of the seas was not among them. My 'ocean' voyages consisted of taking the night boat to Boston. There were two boats run by the Eastern Steamship Line, the City of New York and the City of Boston. Each boat sailed from one of those ports every day and passed each other in the dead of night on the Long Island Sound. It was a wonderful trip for an 'overnighter'. You boarded near the foot of Manhattan. Then you sailed around the tip of Manhattan under the Brooklyn Bridge and the other bridges that connected Manhattan to Brooklyn, and then into the Sound. As you sailed up the Sound you passed the storied houses of millionaires on both sides of the shore.

They were quite a sight, standing in majesty along the shore, hidden from the roads, but seen from the Sound.   Greenwich was on the other shore and they had their share of grandeur too.

The dining room was what you thought all steamship dining rooms ought to be, crisp, and white, full of people celebrating the ride.

These boats were overnighters, the New Haven Railroad also sent an overnighter to Boston, but the boats had a sense of festivity. Certainly they took longer, but no one was in a hurry. If you were on business, you left at the end of the business day either in Boston or in New York, you arrived in either port at the beginning of the business day, so why not a little relaxation in the interim.

There were bars, and after the dining room closed shipboard horseracing. On one of these trips, I won something like ten dollars, which was a fortune in those days for a youngster like me to have. That trip I had my own stateroom, so I was not under supervision of anyone.   Late that night I went up to the upper deck where the funnels were. The ship was quiet except for those hangers on who were drunk and wandering about looking for some sex. It was foggy that night as it was wont to be in Summer time on the Sound, suddenly the ships foghorn sounded. Once again I clung to the rail. It was not as shocking as the Queen Mary, but it was enough to send me straight to bed.

The next day in Boston, the friends of my parents who brought me on the trip, stayed with their friends, and sent me off to the Gardens to ride on the Swan Boats, and generally make myself scarce for a while. I had a fine time, not only riding the Swan Boats but going over to Tremont Street to Schraffts for an ice cream soda. It was a wonderful day, and late that afternoon we once again boarded the same boat we arrived on to go back to New York. It was a one-day event, unimaginable to me, but it contained everything I could ever want in a short holiday, actually I think it was a Memorial Day holiday, and in those days, all holidays were on that day, none of this weekend stuff.

Once upon a time, seeing friends off on a trip to practically anywhere was an event. The steam ships were particularly glamorous. Even if you were in third class in a stateroom the size of a postage stamp, there was still an air of excitement abroad. People brought fruit baskets and champagne, and the stewards brought plenty of ice.

Even if you were sharing a stateroom with a complete stranger, it was fun. Usually there were their friends too, and before you knew it, everyone became 'best' friends.

There was more room in second class, and things were grander. It was considered the middle class way to go, and families who lived in Darien would take a couple of staterooms for the family. A lot of staterooms were on the inside of the ship so there were no portholes.

Most people used the stateroom to sleep in and change for all the various functions on board. Each class had its own territory; dining salon, salon, bar even deck space. Of course, first class had the top of the ship and all the grandeur you could imagine. People didn't mix in the classes. Unless you were invited by first class to visit from either second or, God forbid, third class, you were absolutely segregated. In the sixties Canard stopped all the various parties and boarding of friends before the ship sailed. The Irish problem made security a must. The other lines didn't stop then, but Trans Atlantic travel on a ship was beginning to become passé. Air travel was taking over, even before the jet planes rose to capture all travel, ostensibly. An era was lost to expediency.

Now travel is a much different experience, you are beholden to the air lines time schedules, which can become a variable dependent on the day and circumstances you travel, and though you pay your fare, the attitudes of airline employees is pretty universally bad. But something came out of all that; cruises the opiate of the masses.

Today we fly via cramped quarters to cruises. It is something wonderful; you don't sail from New York any more, but from ports closer to destinations you will travel to, saving days of your vacation.

Once you board ship, wherever you are going, you have those days to actually go to the places cited in the travel guides. The unfortunate thing of course is; you can't spend any time in one place long enough to really get to know the destination of the day. It doesn't really matter in the long run because you have 'gotten some of the flavor' of the place, not the essence.

What has happened, people of modest means can escape to a land on the sea of ultimate luxury. A place where you are 'king and queen' of all you survey at the moment. For as many days as you choose, or can afford, you can strut your stuff. You can be anyone you want. If you have a cabin with a porthole or two, you can be a Duke. If you have a suite with a separate bedroom, you can be rich, and if you have a small stateroom with cramped quarters no one will ever know who you really are if you don't tell them. Your fantasy is yours to hold for as long as the cruise is; it is the world in your hand. Shipboard acquaintances become bosom buddies for the time you are with them. When you disembark, you promise to write, keep in touch, become fast friends, and you do for a bit of time. Then, as memories do, they fade into what we want to remember in photographs, or bits and pieces of what we take with us as baggage and souvenirs for our memories.

Once upon a time, travel was a different style, full of class distinction, money made the line demarcation. Today we have become more and more one society, traveling where we will. You don't know if the person sitting next to you in the cheapest seat in the plane is a pauper or a millionaire. You don't know if the couples you become friends with on a cruise are rich or a poor couple having saved for the trip as a celebration. We have become 'one' when we travel today, no one is better anymore.

The ferryboat has always been one class.

ALWAYS

Jeremy Flagland woke with a start. He had forgotten where he was. He dreamt he was in a very different place in a different time. The thing he remembered was that he was not who he was now, but someone from a different time, and in a different body, but the person was him.

He lay in his bed wondering about all that. Dreams, he had heard, were sometimes prophetic, or answered questions you asked the ether of life, as one of his friends said. He wondered why he found himself a different person in a different place in a different time. He remembered flying high above the earth at times in dreams, and the feeling of elation to soar above the earth.

This was different. He was not in his body, but in a different body, whose? He worked to recreate the dream and found it muddy as it was constructed now. The body was amorphous, without gender it seemed. It gave him pause, but the alarm went off at that moment and he got up for the day.

Jeremy worked for an investment firm. He worked with a man whose job it was to rate and decide what investments the firm would make. He also worked on research for the firm that helped it decide whether they would back new issues of stock. It sounds mundane, of course, but it had its fascination.

It was time consuming, but not brain damaging. When he left work at night the limo picked him up and took him home to his comfortable apartment on East 56th Street. He showered and changed into something more comfortable for the evening.
Usually he met friends and went to one of the East side's trendy little restaurants the Times gave two stars to about three weeks ago. By that time, the super trendy diners would have fallen off and the restaurant would be pleasanter to dine. If the restaurant got three stars, they waited six or seven weeks to dine. What a difference the Times makes!

Jeremy and his friends loved to watch the goings on in places like this knowing they would never catch a wink of attention from the paparazzi so their voyeurism was safe from detection, and there would be no pictures in the New York Post the next day.

He made a very good salary for one so young, just out of school. Jeremy attended two schools simultaneously.   He astoundingly graduated Suma Cum Laude from both, the top Engineering school in the country and one of the most prestigious Music schools.   He was a fine pianist and studying to become a conductor.   Yet he felt displaced in the fast-paced world of finance and after work social times.   There was not a balance.   Jeremy had a girl friend, in the genre of 'girl friend'; his sexuality had been explored so he was not a novice at what he did.

There was no balance.

His looks were elfin, in the sense; he was not large and strapping, but small and finely defined. His face was handsome with a dark shock of hair that kept falling over his forehead.   His eyes were laughing brown and serious grey.   He was quite a catch in anyone's society.

But there wasn't a balance.

He searched for his life. He had said many times the world of finance was not necessarily for him.   He made good money, which he spent quickly. He was young and unformed.   If you can call a fine pianist and genius at mathematics unformed.   What should he do with this, he wondered more than once.   His work only challenged part of him. He felt many things. He never thought of himself as creative, so he did not. There were times he felt he could sense something wanting to jump out of him waiting to be recognized.

The days went on and he worked, and played. He put away any longing he might have felt to dig deeper into himself to find who he was in the fix of things.

There was too much distraction; too much to drink and eat, too much to buy and wear. Always in the back of his mind there was a little voice urging him to go on an adventure, and become his dream.

Ah, but time called again and again to bring him to the table of the real world that fed him. He amassed more and more things, more and more designer clothes he'd wear once, maybe. His life was slipping away from him until he found himself at forty, that ever-dangerous age, not knowing who he was. He was rich, he had a wife, and he had alimony payments and children he sent to first class schools as a badge of honor to his money.

Yes, finance had claimed him, and made him 'its'. Once in awhile he picked up a score and conducted the air. The music on the page before him resonated the sounds of an orchestra as he imagined he would hear it. These were moments of solitude he spent with more Brandy than he liked, but the music came with Brandy. The fantasy came with Brandy. Children were shut out with Brandy, as were alimony payments and financial alliances. Yes he was rich, but not with the wealth of his youth where talent connected him to his soul.

An old friend, who in his twenties was seventy, and now ninety, invited Jeremy to visit him. This man loved Jeremy many years and was dismayed, as his life went on, that Jeremy never held to his promise, but went on to become one of the mundane rich people who no longer reach out of their lives to grasp the hope of the future. The future was theirs, spent in lives that gave no meaning to talents long ago held in hope.

His friend welcomed Jeremy with much love and enthusiasm. They hadn't seen each other in years. Obviously each had changed. Jeremy looked a worn forty plus and his friend looked a youthful ninety. For a man so old he was full of life. The gent was still a good cook and they sat and talked of life for many hours. Jeremy began to feel loss, as he looked at the wilderness of some of the scenery he saw.

His life once green and pure had been taken over by progress and priorities. Jeremy felt his life looked like this; at once a perspective of purity, then, the brambles of priorities. He had so much to support.

One time they were talking on the patio by the pool, dusk was setting in for the night. They each had a drink. The day had been glorious. Jeremy had to think about getting back to New York, life called him to duty there. As he mused he remembered the dream he'd had so many years ago and finally recognized who it was in his dream. It was him. It was him in that other body, an older man, bereft of his dreams in youth, caught up in a world that takes you away if you dare not play its game.

There were others who showed you that all the gold, all the angst life presented to you need not be if you just took the time to wonder at the stars and know that out there was the entire panoply of existence. There, out there was no judgment of your life. If there was anything at all in all those stars, it was hope that what you are blessed with as talent would be used for your eternal future.

Jeremy began to understand what he had done. He allowed the ease of what he had done with his life, and the money to purchase his soul. He asked his friend if this is how he understood life. You are given a creative talent to deal with. To know who you are, at least the beginning of who you are, and follow it to the end? The old man, himself had struggled with his own entity, but knew infinitely more because his years of searching to find that smallest part of his soul, looked at the stars and said, "It is, it is this way, in all the paths of life we take, ...always."

SHE'D BE BETTER IF THEY'D LET HER

Filena Potts rose from her kitchen table and walked slowly to the front door. The bell had rung many times, but she was not in the mood for 'company'. However, the insistence of the bell drew her to the door. She was dressed as usual in a flimsy pink wrap. Filena rarely went out of doors earlier than dusk. Said it was bad for the skin to show it off to the sun. Hers was creamy white and unblemished, the envy of every woman in town. They all had to do work a day things like clean house and garden and expose their skins to the out doors in all weathers. Filena stayed behind closed doors and draped windows. It wasn't as though she was rich, she wasn't. She had enough to live on if she was careful.

Her only 'friends' were gentlemen, lonely gentlemen who were passing through town, so the gossip went. Now this is not what you think right off. Filena was not a loose woman. She was a lonely woman. And because her skin was creamy and clear, and her figure was full and not used as the other womens' in town were, she was somewhat an outcast in society, so to speak. No woman likes to look at another woman and know down deep in her heart of hearts that she could never aspire to looks like Filena's. Well, you most certainly have to dislike a woman like that, mustn't you? You can't invite a woman who looked like that to dinner with other womens' husbands sniffing about the pretty perfume bought in Chicago can you? Nor can you invite her to join the literary club, well of course, it was a small club, not too many women could read further than the Sears Catalogue and that because it was all pictures and they understood dollars and cents.

No, Filena was definitely not a welcome sight when she did sally forth into the dusty main street to the general store late afternoons. She would go there buy her few items and ask if Billy Jordan, the clerk, could carry her bundles home. It was always close to closing time, so old Mr. Dickerdott, winking at the assembled company, would tell Billy to help Filena with her bundles.

Which Billy did with alacrity. He loved Filena. No matter though, he was 'too young' for such a woman as Filena. He was eager to show her all his strengths never the less. They would engage in banter about nothing as they walked to her house. Once there Billy would take the parcels to the kitchen and put them on the table for her. She always offered him a glass of lemonade, which she just happened to have in the cooler under the house. She would bid Billy to go down and fetch the crystal pitcher with all the cut designs on it and bring it up. He did that knowing in his heart she would kiss him. And that did all kinds of things to Billy who was seventeen.

Filena was not unaware that Billy was smitten. She was charmed by it. She also knew he was seventeen. And in a town this small a 'grown' woman flirting with a youth would not be appreciated. I mean, of course, flirting to the point of seduction. After all she was twenty-three and should be married by now. Gentle flirting was always a woman's prerogative. It made men shine, and they go flustery and red. Women like to have that effect on men.

Women like to have their husbands thought desirable by   other women. It makes them feel they'd got a catch. Well, not too desirable, not the kind where there were clandestine meetings behind barns, or anything like that. There was gossip, you know, and that could spread faster than a run away buckboard. And when the dust settled,   WELL!

Filena answered the door expecting one of her gentlemen who was lonely. Imagine her surprise when she saw Billy standing there all smiles with a bunch of his mother's cut flowers. Filena drew her negligee closer and registered surprise seeing Billy. "Why, Billy Jordan. What a surprise seeing you all dressed up with a bouquet of flowers. Are you going off on a spoon date with your girl friend?" "Well, no ma'am, I haven't got no date, ma'am, I came to see you". "My goodness, you came to see me?" "Why yes ma'am, Miss Filena, I was wondering, well I was wondering if I could come in and sit and visit with you in your parlor for a spell." "Well, of course, come right in Billy and do sit awhile. Excuse me for a minute while I change into something more appropriate for a gentleman caller. I can't have you seeing me in my dressing gown. What would the neighbors say if they knew? These are such pretty flowers, Billy, from your mother's garden?" "Yes Miss Filena." "Does your mother know you raided her flower bed to bring me flowers?" "I don't think so Ma'am, she's over at Mrs. Pinckney's makin' a quilt." "Oh, I see, well, lets get them into water so they don't fade.   Come along, Billy you can help me arrange them in water. Get that vase for me will you, the cut crystal one from Chicago, that's it. Now you pump some water in the vase and I'll arrange the flowers".

Billy was beside himself.   Here was the woman he adored arranging his flowers in her negligee. The earth had surely stopped spinning. He pumped some water into the crystal vase. The water was cool as some of it splashed over his hot hand. It momentarily cooled his fever. As he bent over to set the vase on the kitchen table his Lips brushed against her shoulder and he felt faint. Filena was aware of this and she smiled with pleasure. She went to work arranging the blossoms carefully. These flowers to his eye at that moment were the most beautiful flowers ever grown any where on earth. She took each blossom and examined it for a stray bug, after all they were garden flowers, and as she did her negligee slipped open a bit as she moved her arms. He saw her under garment all in white lace with pink roses embroidered on the edge. Her skin was pearly cream white, translucent to look at, and her bosoms heaved ever so slightly as she moved her perfect body.

He was so taken he was breathless and felt his blood rise in every part of his body. His hair literally tingled from the roots. As she placed the last of the flowers in the cut crystal vase, she looked into his eyes with gentle love. "There now, aren't they pretty in water. They like the cool water don't you think Billy?"   "Well, Miss Filena, they are pretty, but not pretty as you are." "Why, Billy, you do have a way with you. Why, I bet when you become a man you will literally sweep the ladies off their feet." "I'm feelin' right manly now Miss Filena, so I must not have too much farther to go to get there." "Well, I can tell you just might be gettin' there at that. You do know that to bring a lady flowers is as close to her heart as when she gets candy or jewelry from a gentleman". "I kind of suspected that miss Filena, and that is why I brought them to you."

They walked back to the parlor and Filena put the flowers on the table near the window where they'd get the light of day when there was some. Billy led her to the horsehair settee and they sat facing each other. Billy sat there real straight and proper. Filena sat next to him looking at him smiling in a warm way, her breasts heaving ever so seductively; Billy was glassy eyed with passion.

"Billy", she said in a thickening voice that spelled trouble, "You are a right handsome boy, and you see, darlin' that's the problem, you are a boy and I am a grown woman, and I'll tell you the truth, I'm twenty-three, I'm too old for you to love". She sat on the edge of the horsehair sofa facing Billy, looking deep into his eyes with desire, and he looked into hers with even deeper desire, and deepest love. His mouth was very dry and his skin was scalding hot, I say scalding because he was perspiring mightily. Her negligee fell away exposing her undergarment and more of her breast. This was almost more than Billy could bear. He heard himself croaking: "Oh Miss Filena I have worshiped at the temple of your beauty since I was twelve. I have longed to be with you like we are just now for so long it pains me to think how much I love you. I know you are twenty-three, but I am grown up in so many ways right now".

"Billy, darlin', you are a grown man in some ways, but you have to do some aging before I could love you". "How much?" "Oh enough so's you would be a man in a man's world, you have to know, how to take care of a lady". "Couldn't you teach me all that? My Ma says you know everything about men and their ways. She says you're an experienced woman in the ways of the world". "Does she say that now? Well my, my, I wasn't aware I had a reputation. Although I suppose a woman, livin' alone without a man does create some chatter around town. I most certainly did not know I was talked about like that!" "Oh Miss Filena I didn't mean to mention such a thing, your past don't mean a thing the way I love you, I can forget about all those other men." "What ever do you mean, Billy? There have been no other men in my life, not a one." "But they say you have gentlemen callers". "Sometimes I do have gentleman callers, but they are lookin' for a wife, not what you and those 'ladies' think. I have been interviewing gentlemen to marry. You see, Billy, when my daddy left me his money and all that stock in Chicago, he wrote in his will that I was to move to this town which was his birthplace, and live in this house until I found me a husband right here. Well I did that, and there are no men livin' here I could marry, well, none I could tolerate, any way, so I put ads in the papers telling men I was interviewing for a husband, and that's how come men visit me".

"Didn't none of them suit you, Miss Filena?" "Nary a one, Billy, they all was lookin' for my money, none of them wanted me. So I have just about give up any hope of ever findin' me a suitable husband, and I'll just have to live here as an old maid all my life on the income that was left me to live here instead of gettin' my full inheritance being a married lady to a man in this town." Billy flushed full red, but he was bold. He got on his knees and looked up into Filena's eyes and said: "Miss Filena, will you marry me, because I love you like nothin' I ever knew before". "But Billy, you're only seventeen, you are just a boy, and I am an old lady, I'm twenty-three, why would you ever want to marry me?" "Because Miss Filena I have been dreamin' about marryin' you for five years".

Filena looked deep into Billy's blue eyes and she knew this was the man for her, a little young perhaps, but he was strapping strong, handsome and ready. Billy was her dream come true. She looked at him, and from his beautiful face on down to his feet, he was what she longed for, he was all she ever wanted. Filena wanted Billy. She would take them both out of this ratty little town forever and she could spend her daddy's money after all.

"Billy, would you like to kiss me?" "Oh yes Miss Filena, I'd just about die to kiss you" "Well, come on then, lets see if you know how." Billy turned toward her and took her in his arms, looked deep into her eyes and gently pressed his mouth on hers. Her eyes closed and her lips parted as did his, their tongues met and they were sweet. Her head fell back into his arms. He kept kissing her. He was a swain of the first order. Filena knew she'd met her man at last. His strong young hands caressed her bosom and encircled her waist like this was something he did a lot.

"Billy" she said with her head still fallen in his arms, "Billy, do you have a girl friend you do this with a lot?" "No Miss Filena, it just comes naturally when I think of you." "Billy, have you ever been intimate with a woman before?" "No Miss Filena I was savin' myself for you." "Since you were twelve?" "Yes Ma'am" "My, my, and what do you think now." "I more than ever want to marry you; I don't care if you are twenty-three. I don't care if you are not a virgin, I love you anyway". Filena sat up quickly pulling her wrap around her shoulders "Not a virgin! Why I am, that was part of Daddy's will I had to be a virgin when I got married." "I'm a virgin too, Miss Filena, maybe that's the way it should be." "But you're seventeen, Billy, you're seventeen, I can't marry you, I'm too old."

Billy took her in his strong young arms again and pressed his lips on hers as if to shut her up, she pushed him away gently. "Billy, if we go on like this we might get into trouble, and do something we might regret later." "Miss Filena, you just let me handle that, you and me are gonna get married when I'm eighteen and its legal, and you'll be a virgin just like you say you gotta be, but we can have a lot of fun in the mean time."

LOVE IS NOT ALWAYS TRUE

Once upon a time there was a handsome young man caught dreaming sitting by the roadside by an old lady. She fancied herself quite beautiful, not having seen her visage in a mirror for many years, she thought of her image as that when she was thirty. The young man looked up at her and his dream vanished before his eyes. He had been dreaming of a beautiful princess who would come upon him, fall madly in love with him, marry him and take him away to Never Never Land For Always.

Imagine his surprise when the old lady came upon him, looked him in the eye and told him she was the Princess Royal and wanted to take him away to Never Never Land For Always. He was quite shaken, to say the least; this was not the princess he had in mind while he was dreaming. 'However' he thought 'an old princess is better than no princess' and, he told himself, he didn't have to spend too much time looking at her anyway. Now, you must understand, the old princess was old, not ugly. And as you looked at her you could see she was well turned out, diamond necklaces tiara and all. The young man, shall we say his name was Gideon, was not above improving his station in life, because he had little to offer anyone, even an old princess, except his remarkable beauty.

Now, to some that is quite enough. Beauty speaks volumes to the beholder. Of course depending how it is distributed. His distribution was remarkable, as we said, very well distributed.

The princess put two fingers in her mouth and whistled. Shortly a great coach appeared with four coachmen and six white horses came trotting around the bend. The princess explained she was picking daisies because she loved daisies. That was the reason she was walking by the roadside when she espied Gideon.

"But enough of that", she told him, "climb into the coach and I will take you home to meet the family." He helped her into the coach, the footman glared at him, after all that was his job. And they drove off amid merry chatter. The more Gideon looked at the old princess the more attractive he found her. He could see she had her finer points to reckon her passable in his mind for whatever she had in her mind for him.   That he was passable in her mind was fairly obvious. She wasn't badly kempt, mind you, she had maids and servants. It was just she never looked into a mirror. You might say her vanity was such she never cared. And she had told herself at the age of thirty the whole thing was going down hill anyway, so why bother.

She had never married, never met a man she thought was enough for her in wit, intelligence, countenance; things that mattered in a mate. In addition, there was no reason for her to marry because she had a brother who took care of dynastic matters very well. That, you see, is why she was the Princess Royal. Of course, she had a name: Mary Katherine Angelina and then Trobotsky, after the rich aunt who left her all the money to pay for coaches, grooms, horses, diamonds, maids and servants and all the rest of it. She was not fond of the name, Trobotsky, so she called herself Daisy, Princess Daisy Trobotsky, and that was how she was known far and wide.

Gideon was all agog.   There he had been dreaming of a beautiful princess, when sure enough, a real princess hoved into view, and as we speak, was taking him off to her palace. Not only that, it wasn't even raining. Most of the time, of course, these things happen in a downpour and everyone looks simply dreadful, even the footmen. But not today, there was Daisy, picking daisies in the bright sunshine. What could be more fortuitous? Except, was she thinking of Gideon as a momentary whim, an amusement? Some one she brought home then tossed aside in the morning? Maybe she would cross his palm with a bag of gold so it wouldn't seem so much a waste of his time, which he had plenty of anyway.   It was simply the specter of being put out in the cold grey dawn with the cat, that kind of thing.

However that was not to worry now. The main thrust of the thing was the moment, not the cloudy future. They rolled on through the countryside, and it seemed an inordinately long way to go just to pick daisies, so he inquired, "isn't this a long way from the palace just to come and pick some daisies?" She replied. "It would seem that wouldn't it, but to tell the truth I came looking for you." "You came looking for me?" Gideon asked not just a bit astonished, "How did you know where to look for me?" She replied; "I just knew one of these days I'd meet the man of my dreams, and so I have." "Isn't that a coincidence" said Gideon, "I was looking for a beautiful princess to take me away to Never Never Land For Always." "Well. You see then", the princess replied, "we have found each other after all." "Except, you are a different princess than I imagined." "Of course I am, as you are different than the man I imagined. The main thing is to realize we both found what we were looking for in different packages. If you can stand an elderly princess," as she kissed him, I can stand a frog!"

THE BEETLE
AND
THE WIDE AWAKE JUDGE

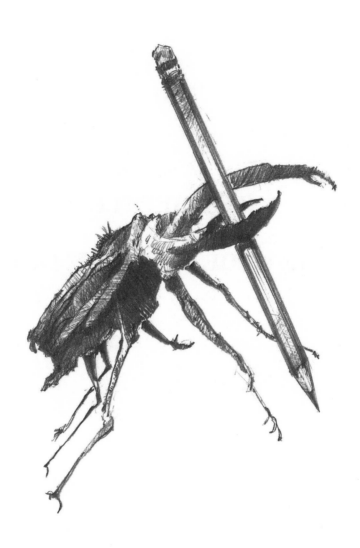

Joe was a beetle, this scarcely makes a difference.

That Joe was a Joe or a Josephine,
I don't know;
For I am not a beetle.

I only tell this story.

I said, Joe was a beetle.

The Beetle Maker put a grain of something extra
in Joe's makeup.
Joe was different from other beetles.

They shunned Joe,
he was an individual;
and
therefore

DIFFERENT

Joe was not physically different.

Actually he was quite handsome...

by beetle standards.

Joe was different because he did not act like a beetle.

Beetles, sense these things,
and though pretty dumb
characters,
being afraid of anything
that is not within their framework to

understand dismiss
that which presents itself being different.

JOE WAS SUMMARILY DISMISSED!!!!!!!!!!!!!!!.

The Beetles Makers grain of something extra was   PERSONALITY.
It must have been.

Joe had PERSONALITY.

UNFORTUNATELY,
it
    was
        not
            beetle
                        PERSONALITY

NOR,
        was it human
                                PERSONALITY

Or dog; Or cat; Or bird, bee or anything else that has

                                PERSONALITY

    peculiar to his species.
                        Actually, Joe thought
                            HE wanted to be human.

He didn't know what a human was.

    HE HEARD THEY WERE THE SUPERLATIVE BEINGS.

        Absolutely in control of everything.

                                Even themselves.

This is a grand thing to be.

Joe decided to be as much of a human being

within his limited beetle framework
as human as he could.

One day,
in the garden where he lived,
Joe came upon some scraps
of food fallen from a table.

It was human food
Carelessly dropped by humans.

Joe,
ambling along the terrace,
came upon them, and ate them.
He found them good to his taste.

After a diet of garden food,
food humans ate was of   particular
delight.

It was different.

When he finished the scraps,
Joe ambled off to rest.

During his sleep Joe decided,
or dreamed he decided,

TO LEAVE THE GARDEN OF HIS BIRTH,

AND TRY HIS LUCK WITH HUMANS.

Human food sometimes makes humans dream strange things.

Think what it must've done to Joe,

unaccustomed to strange morsels.

What Joe dreamed,
only the beetle maker knew.

JOE LEFT THE GARDEN.

No one missed him.
 He was not a part of beetle society,
 and not considered. He could,
 so far as the other beetles were
 concerned
 have to make his way
 as best he could.

 The other members of the beetle community were happy.
Joe was happy.
 He had something,
 He didn't know what.

BUT

it was there.

* *
* *
* *

Judge Henry Brown,

a good pedantic name for a good pedantic man,

was pedantic.

He saw everything straight forward.
He was a Judge,
A good thing too.
For the law is clear.

At least to a Judge.

He was quite able,
when working within the realm of the law.

He epitomized the equal scales of justice.

. . . . . BLIND!

Judge Henry Brown's wife was dull.
Of course she was dull.

She was exactly like all the other Mrs. Henry Brown Characters you
ever knew.
They come in classes.
Every class has them.
Class distinction,

having to do with money
in fact, almost all
to do with money.

It is safe to say:
"All classes of money representation are represented".

Judge and Mrs. Henry Brown were in the middle class.

(No harder class to define. If you are poor, then,

automatically you are in the poor class. If you

are rich, you are automatically in the rich class.

But . . . I defy you to tell me, or find a single

person who will tell you where the middle begins,

and ends)

However;

Judge Henry Brown was a standard in the community.

He Was A Judge.

This gave him standard.

Mrs. Henry Brown reveled in this.

It gave her an edge over the other ladies in the community.

She was:

MRS. HENRY BROWN

wife of the HON. Justice Henry Brown.
She was the style maker.

The ladies' shops where she shopped asked
her opinion of the styles they should stock.
They knew she would buy them.

They knew if she bought them, the other
ladies would too.

She was a leader.

When she decided to go to a reducing salon
for exercise; because it was good for the
figure, the other ladies followed for
the same reason.

(That any of them had anything to
reduce, is quite another question.)

She was a bore.

They all tried to out bore one another.

It was a real challenge; an interesting

game to see who could most interestingly

out-bore the whole group, and see who

could be the biggest bore.

So was he a bore.

However, he was out-bored by the others.

He had no spirit of competition.

Consequently, she,
being a bore
and a style-maker,
and a leader,

other people who followed her in the community
were bores too. Country club golf kind of thing.

It is always safe to play follow the social leader.

One day Judge Henry Brown set off for the Bench.

THE BEETLE AND THE WIDE AWAKE JUDGE 59

T o say it was a different day would not be true.

It wasn't. It was a hot, sunny, summer's day.

The only thing different about the day was the fact
He was not driving to town.

His wife needed the car.

Ordinarily, even SHE would have driven him,
but she had an attack of the Vapors that
morning and wouldn't.

All the other ladies had the vapors too.

(It was fashionable to have the Vapors that morning.

Anyone who couldn't muster an
attack of the Vapors that morning
just wasn't fashionable.

You might wonder how the other ladies knew?
Why, Mrs. Brown called and told them, bright
and early.)

So, Henry took the bus to work.
So did all the other men.

Joe having left the garden
what seemed to be an awfully long
time ago decided to rest.

Beetles move rather slowly when
they are large black garden beetles
with long handsome pincers.

They are formidable looking, but harmless.

Joe thought about climbing a tree to avoid mishap.
He thought about climbing a small tree,
he was THAT tired.

He sidled up to something that was tree-like,
short but shiny. With difficulty
he managed to climb up tree like thing.

                    (It was along the seam
                    of Henry Brown's briefcase,
                    as a matter of fact.)

When he arrived at the top
he found a great gaping hole.

                    (Henry left the briefcase open
                       while he read a brief and waited
                    for the bus)

Joe looked over the edge.

Footing was quite unsure.

He slipped.

He fell.

        Down
                Down
                    Down

THE BEETLE AND THE WIDE AWAKE JUDGE 61

Down,
                    into the
                musty papery darkness.

"My goodness". . . "Life does have its ups and downs".

                    he thought

Joe peered as best he could through the vertical panels   and saw
        daylight.

                SUDDENLY!:

there was a rumble,
                    something narrowly missed him.

SNAP!

        WAVE!

            RUMBLE!

                RUMBLE!

                    RUMBLE!

"My goodness"
            Thought Joe.

"This is a storm. It's night, and I am too warm. I can't sleep with all
this wind and movement."

                The brief case was opened.

        A largish white thing came poking in

and

SNAPPED

up one of the things in the tree.

"I must be doing something human"

thought Joe.

"That looked like part of a human,

but I wonder which part?

Probably a peremptory thing gobbler

that's what it was".

("My goodness,
                I am being jostled,
                                It's most unsatisfactory.

Really, I do think I will go cling to a corner.

                                It may stop then.")

The bus stopped.
The great white thing returned the unfortunate object to its resting place.

"Digested" said Joe

SNAP, SWING and BUMP !

"My heavens, goodness
 and all that, what a whirly-gig this
I am dizzy and awfully tired."

"This world must soon stop moving,
            or I shall be most unhappy."

Soon it did, and Joe slept. Later Joe awakened.

He thought he was in a bee-hive.
He heard bee-like sounds.
It was quite dark where he was.
He pondered whether or not he should move
He pondered he would.

UP

UP

UP

Slowly he climbed
over the lifeless forms
in the world of the briefcase.

He noticed on his way up.
some of the things were missing
from the tree.

 There was more room to move about.
Just to see what would happen,
 he pinched one of the things.

Nothing happened.

'DEAD . . . ALL DEAD. AH WELL THAT'S LIFE'

he thought

there was no corner
and arrived at a place where

top

on

out

climbed

    he

He was still sleepy
And he leaned too far forward,
Z
    O
       O
         O
           O
             O
               O
                 M, M, M M!

                 B U M P !*!*!*

He landed on his pincers impaled in the rug.

"Well" !!!!! "This IS un-dignified".

He waved his legs FRANTICALLY and finally managed to free himself by climbing
              d
               o
                  w
                    n
his pincers.
"Certainly isn't tasty"

                 "TASTY" ???

"I'm hungry'
He saw another tree trunk: (the Judge's leg)
and he started for it.

S*U*D*D*E*N*L*Y
]
The white thing did battle with the tree trunk.

AGAIN!

Vicious thing"

"Must keep out of its way"

He was ascending the new tree trunk.
He found it soft and easily managed.

But then he came to something which lost him.

(The Judge's robe)

Enfolded him.

It moved.
To move a step forward
                              was

            not   to
                        move
                  at
            all.

As best he could he hustled
as quickly as he could
to what he thought
was the top.

                                                UP.
            And that was straight

When he got there he was on top of the world,
except for a peak above him.

The peak didn't look safe to climb,
          it constantly moved and issued loud
                        THUNDEROUS
          noises.

It was safer where he was.

Below him was a plateau
surrounded by three large walls that
contained many objects.
It was obvious the walls held the
objects so they would not fall off.

On the horizon he thought he could make out a sea of movement
doing nothing but
                     Bobbing
                     in place.

He assumed this was humanity.
Now and then one of the ripples larger than the rest seemed to
shoot forward.

             There was much rustling.

Leaves in the wind, some floating to the ground.
The drone of these bee-like creatures increased and decreased,
stopped and went.

Occasionally that creature on whom Joe was sitting rumbled too.

Joe had decided this was no tree but a real live human being.

He decided too, that he was in a gathering of humans.

OH JOY!

What a good time to observe them,
in their natural setting.

He thought the expanse of the plateau below him would be a more
stable place for him to continue his study of humanity.

It looked quite steady.

So
  he
    began
      to climb
        down
          to it.

Judge Henry Brown noticed Joe.

   "What the devil is a beetle doing HERE?"

And then he

   F*L*I*C*K*E*D J*O*E off him

He would have stepped on him too
but the carpet was black.

     The Judge thought
      "Call the exterminators !!! "

Joe was chagrined.

"Most unmannerly of that human, the beetle's

devil take him"

Joe then sat down, crossed his legs and thought.

During his thinking a great flurry of movement occurred.

(The Judge had left)

Everything was very still.
A voice had said:

"Court adjourned until Two P.M this afternoon"

Joe was not familiar with the language sounds of humans and did
not understand.

He sat and thought, and crossed and uncrossed his legs
for a long, long time.

He wondered what to do.

He was awfully hungry, and tired.
He resolved to climb to the top of the plateau again.

  He was so hungry when he reached the top

he would have eaten
anything.

He Slowly made his way up.

BUT,

even

after

a thorough search
there was nothing
to eat.

Even the wood tasted HORRIBLE !!!!!!!

The only thing Joe could think of to do, was sleep.
So he slept.

Later he was wakened by a GREAT LOT of NOISE.

Shuffle, shuffle, scuffle, scuffle, sniffle, brack, kaff, bang!!

(JOE)
(RAN)
(AND)
(HID)

He remembered his last encounter with a HUMAN
and he did not like the idea of being
thrown on the floor again.

The climb up was just too far.

Judge Henry Brown came in and sat on his chair.

Joe noted the human's respect for justice.

There was a lot of shuffling as he (THE JUDGE!!!)   came into the
room.

70   THE BEETLE AND THE WIDE AWAKE JUDGE

(The shuffling was a sign of respect, no doubt.)

Henry moved some papers from his briefcase to his desk,
and put others back.

           The Bailiff called the court to order.
           And thus began the afternoon session.

The day was quite warm. The Judge had eaten a heavy lunch. He
was bored with the cases he had to hear, and decided to let himself
wander.

The smell of new mown grass Warmed by the sun, floated in the
open windows.

For a brief moment, an eternal moment, He was back again. He was
a boy on a summer holiday, visiting a farm, remembering the
sweetness of warm grass.

The summer sounds in the world. They were busy sounds building,
building, and growing, growing. All of life, alive and living. Young
birds toppling about in the air learning to fly, pushed out into life by
loving parent birds, and protected while they learned. Small
animals came to meadow's edge to graze and play and grow.

To learn of life and how to live it watched over by fond mothers and
fathers. All the beings of the meadow and forest lived by the warmth
and growth of the season.

They prepared too, for when it would be cold again.
They Prepared themselves for the dead of winter.

           There was much to be done.

They did it with purpose
warmed by the summer's sun.

The smell of new mown grass.

Henry remembered a Pet Raccoon.
(He'd got him when he was a cub)

The Raccoon was the only pet
Henry had ever been allowed to have.

He was allowed to have the Raccoon,
because a Raccoon was an unusual pet
for a town boy to have.

Henry taught him many tricks.
The Raccoon was shrewd,
and out-witted Henry all
the time.

He could perform a bag of tricks.
He would have performed them all
for a single reward.

Henry gave him a reward for each of his tricks.
The Raccoon became bored with Henry and his games.

And one day he left.

Henry could never guess why.

After all (was his reasoning)

the Raccoon was given everything.

He had to do nothing for what he got.

But, the Raccoon

being tired of the game

simply trotted off

never to be seen or heard of again.

Henry always wondered

WHY?

The smell of summer.
The sound of town,

reminded Henry,
            then a young man away at college
of his aspirations.

He wanted to be a composer.
    Music flowed through him.
        It made him happy.
                    But, he became a Judge
                        because he became a Lawyer.

(A natural sequence of events)

His father was a Lawyer and a Judge.

T R A D I T I O N One never broke T R A D I T I O N

Even though one has 'aspirations'

"Tut tut young man
music is all very well and good.
We need composers, but you are not to be one.

THE BEETLE AND THE WIDE AWAKE JUDGE 73

It could not happen in our family.

(harumph kaff)

BUT,

YOU must become a leader;
your father is a leader.
Your family leads, and produces leaders.
So Henry became a leader.

EVERY so OFTEN he WANTED to BREAK the CHAIN

And do what would make him happy.

"But," "If I had, what would people have thought?
he thought

"There were so many ifs and buts, anything I would've done
would've been relative to what people would've thought."

Once your life's role is accepted
you play it through

and keep your wishes
for cold winter evenings.

It will be then they will light up and keep you warm,
and will become real even for a moment.

"Ah, lovely fantasy.
No matter
I couldn't have done it.

I wouldn't have let myself.

I am not so strong.

So,
Here I am
a musing Judge
on a summer's day

with the smell of new mown grass
Flinging back the memory."

And the memory.

Henry stared glassy eyed out into space.
As he ended his escape his focused on something on his desk. He
came sharply into focus,
disbelieving what he saw.

"My God, THAT is a beetle!"

he thought "What is it doing?"

(Joe was standing on his hind legs waving at the Judge)

"He is waving at me, how wonderful,
no bug ever waved at me before".

(Joe found a pencil on the Judge's desk and began to wave it at him)

"This is delightful, a trained beetle."

(Now Joe danced on his hind legs for the Judge.)

"What a pet, I'll keep him."

(Joe was now holding the Judge's pen in his pincers while he rolled
the pencil with his back legs as a lumberman rolls a log in water.)

This is too good. I wonder if he is hungry?"

(The Judge dug into his desk drawer
and found a package of
peanut butter crackers.
He opened them and broke
a piece off the cracker
for Joe.)

(Joe smelling the first
thing that smelled like
food, fell off the pencil
and tripped over the pen
in his rush for it.)

"He is hungry."

When Joe ate all he could
he burped a beetle burp
and felt better.

(He ate very fast.)
Plans began to form in the Judge's mind.
He knew he had a friend

Now

(A bug, to be sure
but such a bug)

This was the exception in friendship every person has.

(What man do you know, even yourself
who has not had, at some time in his
life, a friend who is the exception

to all your class standards,
even your own?)

(Men are not alone in the exception
 Of having such friends,
Women
and even children do.)

Therefore,
it is justifiable that
pedantic Henry should have
his "ticky" friend too, or
as in this case, his

BEETLE FRIEND!

So it was quite summarized:
Henry had a beetle, a bug, for a friend.

Joe too, was elated.

He could not think of one other beetle who had a real
live human for a friend.

OH

to be sure
beetles had friends,
but not out of
their society.

It was just out of the question.

Now, you and I may look upon this relationship with a peculiar eye,

but, even we must remember, these two, quite outside the realm of
ourselves, in every way,
(and I would ask you this question to prove my point):

Are you on intimate terms with any beetles and Judges?
Or judges with beetles as friends?

Of course not, and not likely to be either.
Under these circumstances the association
was quite acceptable, and natural.

Finally the day was over.

The Judge dismissed his court until another day.

He put Joe in his pocket:
his breast pocket, near his heart.

Joe promised himself and all the beetle Gods
to be the very best beetle friend his friend could have.

Henry promised himself to be the most loyal Judge friend his beetle
friend could have.

This friend had removed Joe (him)
from life in the garden to the wonderful life of humans.

Oh such a friend was this.
Oh such a friend.
How much was his gratitude

we could never know,
except out of our own bursting hearts
full of gratitude and happiness
for something that has made us truly happy.

When the Judge got to the garden gate he put the beetle on his
shoulder.

His wife
over the vapors, dressed in a cool summer frock,
came to the terrace to greet him.

She pecked him on the cheek carefully and murmured:
"Hello my dear, you look tired, and hot, how was your
day?"

She noticed Joe on his shoulder and moved to brush him
off.

The Judge stopped her, he told her about Joe.

As he told her, her face grew, cold with disbelief
her eyes narrowed in disgust; her mouth became grotesque with
distaste; her nostrils flared with contempt; her hair bristled with
loathing; her hands clenched with anger;
her entire being was a sea of vitriol.

(She was quite afraid)

AND

When at last she spoke,
she said in a sweet voice so evenly calculated to destroy
and arsenic sweet:

"But, * my dear,* he* is,* only,* a bug."

The Judge knew, he always had: that one only dreams,
fantasy is not reality, all the hopes, the castles, the aspirations, the
good of oneself, the entire freedom and glory of man's inner
expression, is crushed in fear by men without eyes or heart.

He knew now, that even a friendship with a bug,

a harmless creature,
would be impossible.

The Judge had chosen his role and now must live it
by the rule.
He flicked Joe off his shoulder,
and to make sure no man would succumb
or fall under the spell,
crushed Joe under his heel.

THE END!

BORDERING ON THE TRUTH

Baby LeRoy was three. He lived in a rural community in the late Nineteen Twenties. He had a father who went to work every day at the hardware store in town. His mother stayed home and kept house taking care of baby LeRoy and his father, big LeRoy.

One afternoon, in late summer, his mother put him in the large yard to play. He had no brothers or sisters, so he had to make up games to play by himself.

He had developed an imagination. He remembered stories his mother read to him at bedtime and imagined all sorts of things from them; dragons and castles, maids and soldiers, cats and dogs, and whatever he could imagine he did.

They had a dog; he was an old deaf dog that had been his father's dog when he was growing up. His parents promised Little LeRoy a dog of his own when old Tige went to heaven. Until then little LeRoy had to be content with Tige as his friend. This particular afternoon old Tige was in the house napping beside Little LeRoy's mother's chair. She had decided to sit a while and darn socks, but soon fell asleep, caught up in the summer heat. She planned to make lemonade later for the three of them, his father, LeRoy and herself. In those days people had ice boxes. These were insulated chests that were kept cold with a block of ice that was brought by the ice man on Monday and Friday. This was Wednesday, and when she looked she saw there was enough ice to last until Friday, and there looked to be enough for a piece that could make some cold lemonade. She had bought some lemons and wanted to use them before they went bad. There was much to look forward to that afternoon.

Well, little LeRoy was playing in the sunshine when suddenly an eagle swooped out of the sky and snatched little LeRoy right up in his claws and with difficulty flew away. Little LeRoy was so surprised he didn't even cry out. All he could do was look down as the house and yard grew smaller and smaller. The eagle flew further and further away from the yard. Little LeRoy, of course, couldn't understand what was happening, all he knew was that he was flying up in the sky.

About a half mile away Farmer Brown and his sons were haying. The big hay wagon was standing still with two large work horses at ease munching grass contentedly. The farmer and his sons would swoosh their pitch forks with a steady rhythm picking up huge forks full of cut hay and with a mighty sweep of their arms would toss the hay onto the wagon. The whole thing was like summer music; swoosh, toss, swoosh, toss. The birds chirped in the air as they flew from one tree to another. The eagle found his load of Little LeRoy heavier than he bargained for, and simply dropped him for being too
ungainly to carry further. Luckily for little LeRoy, the eagle dropped him squarely on the hay wagon. He landed with a thud. The horses took note of this strange occurrence, looked up and saw the eagle and panicked. They made a dash for it. Luckily the gate was open and they dashed out on to the country dirt road, turning in the direction of little Leroy's house. The farmer and his sons dropped everything and started running after the hay wagon with all its hay. They were yelling as they ran after the wagon. They finally caught up to the wagon and brought the horses to a standstill. Little LeRoy slid off the hay and on to the ground with a thud. Farmer Brown was amazed and wondered how in the world he got onto the wagon.

He surmised LeRoy had gotten out of the gate and walked through the fields to where he and his sons were haying. He thought too, that LeRoy had been playing in the hay and a son simply 'swooshed' him up with a forkful of hay and threw him onto the wagon. He felt very lucky and that the son had swooshed and not forked him up,
because that would hurt the little boy. What had happened to him was an amazement. So he just stood there and watched the farmer and his sons turn the wagon around and head back to the field. Farmer Brown told LeRoy, he shouldn't walk away from his yard because the big world was out there and he wasn't old enough to understand it all, and to be a good boy and obey his mother. Farmer Brown's sons led the horses and hay wagon back to the field.

About this time little LeRoy's mother woke with a start wondering how long she had been asleep. She looked at the clock and found she had dozed off for about a half an hour. She went to the window and looked out to see LeRoy standing by the gate staring down the road. Her mind was easy that all was well with her little boy. It was a warm summer afternoon, and she just knew nothing had happened while she had her little nap.

She called LeRoy into the house to give him some milk and a cookie. He came in beginning to become excited. He wanted to tell his mother his great adventure. His mother poured him some cool milk and gave him a cookie. He sat down and his mother inquired what he had been doing that afternoon. His eyes grew very big and round and he said: "Oh, Mommy, I was playing in the yard and suddenly this big, big bird flew over and the chickens ran into the hen house. I looked up and saw this big, big bird right above me, and all of a sudden he came down and picked me right up and flew off with me in his feet. I was so surprised I couldn't yell or nothing. We flew over the fields and suddenly he dropped me on Farmer Brown's hay wagon, and he flew off. He must have scared the horseys because they started running all around and on the road. Farmer Brown caught the horses and they stopped and everything. Then I fell off the wagon, and Farmer Brown picked me up and put me over the fence. What do you think of that?"

His mother picked him up and sat him in her lap and brushed his hair out of his face, the way mothers do, and she laughed a little and said: "My, my, what a story that is, you have a great imagination for such a little boy. But you must always tell the truth, or people won't believe what you tell them." LeRoy said: "But, mommy, it happened, it truly did." His mother said: "But LeRoy, there aren't any birds around here big enough that could pick up a little boy like you. You are imagining all this happening to you... ."

"There isn't even any hay on your overalls, so how could all this happen?" "But mommy, its true, its true, I wouldn't tell you a story, you said that is not nice, and you told me I wouldn't go to heaven if I told fibs" "Alright, my darling little angel, it sounds a bit impossible, but if you say so...., now why don't we go into the yard and catch that old rooster and have him for dinner." "You mean old Charlie?" "Yes, that's the one." "But he is my friend, I couldn't eat him." His mother assured him that when she was done with old Charlie LeRoy would never know the difference. And besides, there was a young rooster, and Charlie didn't like him at all, so one of them had to go, and it may as well be old Charlie.

LeRoy's mother was out back dispatching old Charlie when farmer Brown stopped by with some corn and some peaches from his garden. LeRoy ran to get his mother, and she came to the gate where farmer Brown waited. He offered her the corn and the peaches and she said "Why, farmer Brown, how kind and neighborly of you to bring us corn and peaches." "Well, mam" he said "this time of year we have lots more than we can ever use, so why not be neighborly. And isn't it more blessed to give than receive?" "It certainly says so in the bible, sir."

"Did your young'un tell you his adventure not so long ago?" "Why no, farmer Brown, tell me about it." "Well, the boy here seemed to wander off into our haying field. He must have been playing in the hay and we didn't notice him, and one of my sons must have just swooped and picked him up on the fork, and tossed him onto the wagon we were loading. I guess an eagle must have flew over 'bout that time and startled the horses, 'cause before you could say Jack Robinson they were off bellowin', and runnin' away. We finally caught them right in front of your place, and your boy, here slid down off the wagon just as spry. So, I was concerned he was alright." "Why, thank you farmer Brown, LeRoy knows he's not allowed to go away from the yard unless I, or his father are with him, isn't that right LeRoy?" "Yes Mam" "Well. I guess you'll just have to go to bed without your supper for going out of the yard."

Farmer Brown, a generous man, said: "Oh, don't be too hard on the young fella. These peaches are mighty good and ripe, and with some cream on them they'll make good eating. Not to mention the corn, and this time of year's fresh tomatoes. Why that corn slicked up with butter an' some good chicken Fricassee . . ." "Why Mr. Brown how'd you know we were having chicken tonight?" "Didn't, Ma'm, just sounded good, my wife's fixin' chicken tonight, I just guess that's where I got the thought." LeRoy said, sounding hopeful "My Ma's gonna cook ole Charlie the rooster, aincha Ma?" "Well, LeRoy, I just guess I am, just like Mr. Brown said, I'm going to make us a Fricassee." "Best thing to do" farmer Brown said, "only way to get an old bird tender, my wife says."

Farmer Brown took his leave and said, "Now ma'am, don't be too hard on the boy, you know, boys will be boys, they love to explore, and have adventures. Wait'll you have a couple more runnin' around you'll sure have your hands full then." "You are probably right, Mr. Brown, thanks again, and please remember me to your wife. Come along LeRoy, let's clean up the feathers from ole Charlie, and then begin dinner." "Do I have to go to my room, Ma?" "No dear, for a little boy who's had such adventures you're sure to be hungry. Pick up that bag of corn and peaches and take them into the house, then come out to the hen house, that's a good boy."

Old Tige woke up about now and came to greet LeRoy wagging his old tail happily. He came up to LeRoy to give him a good smell. All of a sudden he gave a low growl as if all was not right. LeRoy reached up and put the peaches, tomatoes and corn on the kitchen table and ran out the door with old Tige in hot pursuit. He was barking following LeRoy. His bark was not that of playing, but of warning. When LeRoy got to the hen house, his mother was cleaning up the old Charlie's feathers. The hens were aroused with all the commotion so LeRoy's mother didn't notice that old Tige was making such a fuss.

LeRoy, his mother and old Tige went into the house. Old Tige was calmer now that he had done his job and warned everyone of something he knew wasn't right. They all knew, and the danger he was barking about seemed to be past.

Well, sure enough they had Charlie fricassee, and corn, and tomatoes from the garden, peaches and cream and lemonade. Little LeRoy was full right up to the top. His father asked him what he had done that day. Little LeRoy recounted his adventures. His mother mentioned the visit of Farmer Brown. LeRoy's father admonished him to stay in the yard unless he was with him or his mother. Little LeRoy didn't know what to think. He knew what had happened to him, but couldn't get anyone to believe him. He just knew he had to keep it to himself forever as his own adventure, but suppose the eagle had not dropped him on Farmer Brown's hay wagon, what then? Suppose the eagle had flown far far away, what then? Wouldn't they believe him then? He went to sleep wondering why no one believed him.

Later when his parents turned off the lights and were going to bed, LeRoy's mother said; "Dear, I think it is time for LeRoy to have a playmate" LeRoy's father reacted kind of startled; "You mean get rid of old Tige? Why I've had him since I was a boy, you can't mean that? Can you?" "Why no, silly" she laughed, "I mean he should have a little brother or sister" LeRoy's father's face brightened considerably, as he took his wife's hand and led her up the stairs. She stopped him for a moment; "Let me check LeRoy and make sure he is alright" her husband kissed her on the cheek and went into their bedroom. LeRoy's mother went into his room. Everything seemed in order, old Tige was sleeping at the foot of the bed and woke momentarily and when he knew who it was thumped his tail a couple of times and went back to sleep. She picked LeRoy's overalls up off the floor, and as she did old Tige woke up and sniffed the air and growled. She felt something on the back suspenders, it felt like holes and the fabric was slightly torn. She knew LeRoy hadn't done any thing like that to rend his overalls. What could it be?

Pondering the possibilities, she shut the door to a crack and went in to her waiting husband. Nevertheless, it was a ponder. Were eagles that large?

THE MAN WHO LIVED
IN THE TRESTLE BRIDGE

For

ANTHONY HOPKINS

When you drive down the Keys to Key West, there is a new highway to drive it. The old highway runs alongside in places; the new highway is a white ribbon surrounded by blue and sea foam green waters.

There is a bridge called "Seven Mile Bridge". It is not a span bridge, but a road over the waterway built on pilings. As you drive down the Keys, just beyond Seven Mile Bridge, to your left are the remains of the railroad bridge built many years ago by Mr. Flagler. His railroad ran all the way to Key West and was really the main road from Miami. The 'street' road was, until the new road was built, a narrow two lane road that could be slow, to say the least.

Looking at the railroad span you'll see it was once a trestle bridge. It is steel on pilings and severed at either end because "they" don't want you to go from the spit of coral reef at one end or from the key at the other end, and walk or fish or play in the trusses.

One day driving down I looked across the water at the bridge. It was a slow driving day and I could gaze leisurely at it. It is an amazing relic to earlier technology, all that steel carried so long ago from Miami to Key West.

As I studied the bridge, I thought I could see some movement in the girders near the water. 'What is it,' I wondered; 'some children who rowed out to fish or explore?' But there didn't seem to be more than one person in the framework of the structure. I drove on.

When I driving north a few days later I looked again, as I always do, at the trestle bridge. Once again I thought I saw movement there. The traffic was faster that morning light plays strange tricks on water. Maybe I saw nothing.

It stayed in my mind.

Had I seen someone in the trestle bridge? I wasn't going to contemplate it that much, it certainly wasn't a priority piece of thinking, but it stayed on my mind.

Some weeks later when I drove south again, I attempted to ignore the trestle bridge. As it appeared on the horizon, and I approached I slowed and looked. It was a bit late in the day and I fancied I saw something. Up in the roadbed I thought I saw something white; it couldn't be a play of light. It had form, so it wouldn't be fabric caught in the steel somewhere.

It had form.

I was having dinner with friends during that stay and I mentioned, casually as I could, that I kept thinking I'd seen someone in the bridge. Had anyone else had that experience? "Why yes," I was told, "there is rumor someone lives in the bridge, within the trusses; but it is widely believed it is a myth. How could someone live, actually live within the trusses of a trestle bridge?" Well, I found, if there is some mystery about it, I must find out.

It did not hold me captive, but I knew somewhere in the back of my mind, I must find out what was there.

It was a holiday time later, about six weeks or so. As usual, we had guests. Most of the time I don't mind having people. Most of them are perfectly nice, and if you are very smart, you can ignore them and go about the business of keeping a garden going.

Since the reason to come to Key West, (for most of the people I know anyway,) is to relax, swim, and sun. Regardless of what is said about getting a tan, tans are got to great triumph. Of course, the scum in the pool from sun tan lotion is pretty disgusting. Oh, what the hell, it is part of the game of having fun and being a guest.

It is not a long trip by boat to go from Key West to where the bridge is. In the Keys where the weather is clemency itself, it is rather a pleasure to sail north. As usual, a blue blue sky with an occasional cloud scudding through eases the constant sun from the deck of the boat and off exposed body parts. A now and then shower can be a blessing. You don't get really wet, just sprinkled on as you go north.

If you are sailing, the windward breeze is usually enough to carry you along at a good speed.

Which is one of the good things about the Keys; there is always a breeze blowing through, and even in ninety-degree weather, it is not hot to the point of being unpleasant. Humidity is another thing; being surrounded by water, it can be quite apparent.

I was alone in my boat, unusual for me, there are always travelers to be with, but I had slipped away easily and was out of earshot when I looked back at the dock at waving arms signaling me to return for the rest of them. I sailed on, determined not to look back or feel guilty for not including them in this adventure. It was my day.

I felt recently I'd not had time alone and wanted to simply take this as my own. I planned to have an adventure that was not inclusive of anyone else. Nor would they understand my desire to sail to the trestle bridge and have a look around.

Every day is perfect in the Keys, somehow even, rainy days. There are days when rain clouds dance around the sun and shower places for moments, then blow themselves away to another place to repeat their performances. To have more than a couple of days of truly inclement weather is unusual. The Keys escape all this because the trades blow north, up over Florida from the Gulf of Mexico. It is rare to have a nor'easter that sticks. Even then, it has benevolence about it. The weather seems to say, "We need the water" and we get it. Roofs leak and Key West's streets flood in unexpected ways, the sewers, unused to torrents, plug up and become ponds when they can't run off, and the people grumpily make do with nature's word.

Of course, when a 'big blow' is expected, everyone prepares for the blow. Nothing like thirty-five has happened in years, and the Keys, flat as they all are, seem immune to the drenching from large storms. They roll over the Keys and the Keys survive to see the sun shine again. The blooms freshen themselves in the sun and show all their color.

Even when Miami is forty degrees, the lower Keys escape cold weather for the most part. The Bahamas are kin to Miami weather-wise, and have some very chilly days.   Key West is special because of its mystique, which is: it is the most southerly point of the lower forty-eight States.   It might be fair and true to say that every visitor to Key West has stood and seen the marker, telling all this is 'it'.   Undoubtedly millions of snapshots proclaim the subject to be not so much the portrait of the 'tooken' as having stood there.

Key West is a place where fantasy can become real if you close your eyes. Reality is always seen through closed eyes. The notion of going through your life with your eyes wide open is a metaphor for divining reality being there only in that prospect.

My day's sail began early. It is not far to the trestle bridge as the crow flies or the ribbon road goes, but it is several hours by sail. I could have motored and got there sooner, but the day was perfection. The breeze was right. My boat is simple enough, a forty footer. We can sleep six and often have, and the boat can be sailed alone, if you are a sailor, and my experience is there.

The day sparkled the water did too. Even the boat responded as though it were alive.   Well, boats are alive, true sailors know this deep in their bones; a boat is a living thing. For some, an automobile lives, it doesn't; maybe a few vintage cars have tales to tell and were made by men who loved them, who nurtured them from metal to shape to speed through beauty. Lines were rakish and you were somebody in a 1934 Cadillac four-door phaeton 16 cylinder in line double v-eight. A Packard of that vintage, or Rolls-Royce or Bentley all names of famous cars roll off history with beauty and grace. Today only Jaguar seems kin to the spirit of grand automobiles, and that is moot.

So it is with sailboats.   Because they are, in essence, so in tune with the water they sail, even the simplest 25 footer has the majesty of the sea at its helm. They sing you know, a happy sailing boat is a chorus of chimes and creaks and grunts.

Unfortunately, fiberglass boats are not as musical; progress wends its way to ruin everything, even sail boats. The slap of water against wood has resonance no man made element can compete with; mine is fiberglass. Sorry.

I will never forget a trip through the Windwards aboard a 75 foot charmer. My God what elegance! She fit the sea like a glove. You could tell they were friends, made for each other. Teak and Honduras Mahogany blended to an elegant shape no man could resist.

The boat sailed with the majesty of the Normandie or Queen Mary, (same vintage), well and lovingly cared for by a succession of owners who knew her worth. No one sailed that boat who did not fall in love with the sea, and would never have left her had their time with her not been over. That boat was a loving mistress to all men who loved the sea she sailed. Perfection and all elements bowed her way. She sails still, majestic as old as the Normandie or Queen Mary, but not abused as they have been. She commanded you love her, and you did.

Since then there have been no 'ships'; the last was the France, now put to sail as a cha-cha boat promising much. Ships today are sailing tenements with deck on deck of stateroom warrens for weeklong fantasy seekers on a vacation they never could afford to live otherwise. Dignity has left the sea, look what we have done to it and you will know we are not worthy of all it is; life to man.

Did I muse these things as we sped up the Keys to the trestle bridge? Probably I did, being my age and remembering the past, I wonder, sometimes, how old you must be to remember the past; not old I think.

The breeze sped us on up the Keys. I looked toward shore and saw the houses nestled white in the green palms. People were at breakfast, it was about that time. The waters were awakening with powered boats carrying fishermen out for the catch of the day. A sunfish or two played in the shallows.

I am continually surprised how people take to water, especially warm water; you can't seem to keep children away from it. The youngest children are of the sea, natural to the water as fish would be, would one say; mermaids? mermen? merchildren?, not formed to become, anything but natural to their surroundings.

The saltwater of the Keys is sweeter than the salt water of Maine or California; perhaps sweeter than anywhere on earth. If salinity is a gauge, it is probably really the same anywhere. More than likely it is sweeter in other respects of the imagination.

You can fantasize anything from a distance. Look from hill to hill and wonder what is in the valley. If you see farms, villages, animals, it all looks innocent.

Yet we are beginning to know that all the view from far away is as far from the truth as the place we look. From the air the neat patches of farm, with borders of fences and roads look pristine. Towns laid out, straight streets, cross roads, from one end sparse settlement to the other, show order in the context of the place.

Ultimately, what is order from afar?

When you sail in a sailboat, mechanical things seem to come to you unconsciously; that is if you know how to sail a boat. Those who are not real sailors always seem to fidget; getting it right. A sailor accustomed to his boat, sails as it feels, conscious he has done the maneuver called. It lets him muse far beyond, being sedentary. One moves thoughts; they move from dot of introspection to the realm of great ideas. I'm sure writers like Hemingway plotted their stories as they moved through where they were. It allowed space for creation in thought.

The waters of the Keys are sparkling blues and greens, as a perfect Aquamarine is in color. The sun dances off the water giving it a golden cast. In the distance are low mounds of green, like English muffins, green muffins. They are islands, mostly uninhabited because there is nothing to inhabit. Now and then you see a structure at the side of the sea, someone has laid claim to a muffin of the sea. I've never ventured close to an island with a shack. As I understand it, some are quite substantial. In which case one has to presume there are amenities.

Amenities being a practical presumption of a substantial house but one never knows.

All kinds of thoughts ran a course through my mind that morning, none more prevalent than my journey itself. It was self-indulgent and totally without reason. Who takes his sailboat, alone, and sails thirty miles north to see if someone lives in a trestle bridge?
Others might think there is a fine madness here, and there is; shall I turn about and head home? "Well, you've come this far, you may as well prove your point." Is there someone in the trestle bridge? On the other hand, is it your imagination? Logic, ever confounding fantasy, would say; how could anyone live in the trestle of a bridge? Logic would say it is impossible, just from the viewpoint of possibility. How does one live in the span of a bridge without being taken off by the authorities or hounded by the people who live on either shore of the span. The cut made from either shore is not so far from land that people could not row, even swim to the bridge, so it is not isolated, as it seems. I don't know, but it stands to reason: the bridge span is the kind of place curious people would investigate. It is not far away from Route One north and south, a half mile perhaps, clearly visible from the road. A driver might not, but a passenger could study the frame and would, more than likely, see a person in the structure. Those people on shore would notice movement in the steel girders and beams. No, logic tells me no one would, or could live in that bridge.

Most assuredly, people visit the structure, fish from it, around it. Children, oh not little children, but ones old enough to be agile and large enough to climb the girders, could do that, if no one objected. Even if they did, so what. Young people know better and will do what they please to a great extent, consequences be dammed.

The fantasy of it all is that the trestle bridge is remote in my mind. The land is close in reality. In this fantasy as far away as the muffins I pass sailing by.

The span is standing like a sculpture in the sea, not unlike, really, the oilrigs in the North Sea we passed on a cruise some years ago.

The rigs were massive structures, perpendicular to the ocean, which was calm then at the time. Standing on legs like storks, four legged storks to be sure, maybe more legged, but the rigs were remote to us on the ship. We took pictures of the rigs and thought we saw people waving; maybe we did. We waved back, perhaps at no one. I looked at the rigs and thought, "these are the universe to these people who live and work on them." To be sure, for the time they are there, they are. Looking at them, remote and distanced from all the others, this ship and the land beyond made each one singular, with its own society and pecking order.

Realistically, they were connected as could be with each other, with land, even with this ship. These people had television, phones, radio, electricity, heat, air-conditioning, if need be; they were connected in every way by the umbilical cord of communication and attached to the land of the sea floor. Yet they were worlds unto themselves and in that respect, remote from it.

Remoteness is as close as the person next to you in a moving vehicle. Shoulder to shoulder you sit in your own world, they in theirs. You touch, not noticing the humanity of the bump, no need to excuse yourself, it is understood; the train, plane, bus jostled you and them to bump. It happens.

I have thought much about how remote we have become from each other. On a singular note, I, from my family, friends, people I work with. I am more connected to the shopkeeper because I am forced to communicate what I want, and in doing so, pleasantly as possible. I don't want to be thought a grouch, even though I may be grouchy that moment.

Hiding my feelings from my family, working to cope with them, as I cope with my life (my personal down deep life) I don't understand. I wonder how many of us know who we are in relation to our selves, our lives, our existence.

I know no on who can answer that, there are so many variables. We judge our lives by variables and we live our lives as if life were meant to mean stationery to movement within ourselves. We are not permitted movement beyond certain limits we have chosen/made by choice or circumstance ultimately we live within confines of our choosing. We may chafe at the rein and bit we find ourselves haltered in, but the bit in our mouth controlled by circumstance we give rein to, become our path to death.

No one reads our thoughts. The idiot thinks. No one reads our dreams. The blind dream in vision they understand. No one hears our cries for love. Our dogs are more petted than we.

No one yearning to existence to become, they cannot realize our cries of pain; theirs are too great to hear us, ours too great to notice theirs, and all of us adrift to the end of time we shall never know.

Perhaps these are thoughts of a boatman alone sailing to visit an idea a notion in the Florida Keys.

Perhaps they are thoughts similar to a person circumnavigating the globe, alone when you are alone, alone, your destiny literally in the hands of existence.

For me the journey was not that far away. I could see land, houses, the ribbon of bridge continuing the road north and south. The boat was being good to me as was the breeze. We sped along, I guessed about seven knots; there was a slight chop to keep me from dreaming too much. What else was there to do? You can indeed reach for the stars even when they don't shine above.

I seemed to be coming near to the trestle bridge area. I'd never sailed here before, so it was by sheer instinct I even began to know where I was. Traveling the Keys in a car gives you an entirely different perspective than sailing, obviously, as did going by plane. I hadn't brought a chart, I really didn't know why, other than I habitually forget 'something' almost every time I drive off. Most often, it is my glasses. I forget grocery lists, directions to a strange place I will visit, the phone number of the people I will visit. In other words being "methodical" is not my thing. It didn't matter anyway, if I had a chart I couldn't read it, of course: No glasses.

I have tried to keep a pair of glasses in every room in the house, even a pair in the boat, certainly in the car. The pack rat in me puts glasses down, now in that spot, pick something up, maybe answer the phone, maybe, or move from place to place. Then I have to retrace my steps all the way back to find the glasses where I put them, maybe. Thank God they are "drug store" bought and can be had for $12 a pair, losing a pair, seriously losing a pair doesn't hurt as much as losing a pair of bifocals, say, but nonetheless, losing a pair of glasses is cause for much annoyed groaning.

No chart, no glasses. Just the seat of my pants as it were. I knew if I sailed close to shore and follow the general topography of the Keys; sooner or later I'd reach the Key where the bridge is located.

The Key south of the bridge is the Key where the endangered Key Deer are. There is a lot of hullabaloo about whether or not developers should be allowed to gut the Key and to hell with the deer. The consensus so far is to hell with the developers; but as in all things progress will probably win, money being far more important than Key Deer. Just these things make me wonder, from time to time, is it all worth the while?

Thinking, thinking, thoughts, thoughts, enough to make a person contemplate a global circumnavigation. It isn't just the lure of the trip; it's the thinking. Being alone is having no one contradict you or affirm your view. It is suspension, unless you are visited by a deity with instruction, and that seems unlikely.

The seat of my pants paid off; and there it was. Not much maybe, just by eye, the bridge seemed to be about two hundred feet long, cut at each end. The distance to shore a hundred feet from at either end.

You could swim to it, or from it. The trestle sat on pilings of concrete that were anchored for the roadbed of what had been track for the trains.

Unlike a sculpture, made to weather the elements, erosion of the metal showed. It is not a maintained monument to Mr. Flagler's bold venture of running a train to the Keys, which when you think about it, was boldness and initiative at its American best.

Given the times in which it was built, it was a great feat. Undoubtedly building trestles across great chasms as the railroad wound west in earlier days were in themselves great feats to ingenuity and initiative. This railroad still ranked with them though built a half century later.

I wish I had made the trip. It would have had to have been before the great hurricane of 1935 which blew the dream away beyond repair.

This was the last vestige of this particular empire, and no one ever had the dream to rebuild. Now there are new ribbons of road over the Keys, and trucks bring all there is from the mainland in big rigs, day in and day out. It could be done more simply by rail. In this day of ecological awareness, a train would pollute about a hundredth what cars and trucks do.

As I approached the bridge, I dropped the sails with intentions to take them in entirely and proceed slowly under power. As the boat moved toward the span I searched the girders for something, someone. I don't know, why even now, but I was drawn to this place for some reason beyond my realization. There was nothing there to make me believe there was anyone lurking, much less, anything that would indicate a place where one could live.

The bridge was not hospitable to the notion that one might find a home there. I couldn't sail under the trestle, for my mast was too tall, but could see light streaming through the metal beams.

The water played with sunlight to cast shadows that could be anything a flight of imagination made it.

I looked for concrete evidence, a stable form, something with density fleshed out to be human, or what I thought should be.

Light played with my fascination in it; there seemed to be nothing rooted in fact. Yet there was this feeling, if you will, there was form, as I imagined it, lurking in what shadow there could be, call it intuition.

There was no one in evidence in the bridge. Slowly I motored the length of it and peered hard to find some sort of movement in the span. Nothing was there, and yet my intuition told me there was something.

It was getting on in the day and I decided to try again another time.

I turned into the wind and raised my sail. It is not a tricky business, getting under way, but it is a methodical kind of thing. As I secured the last line and the sails were steady and the boat began to move away, I glanced back at my adventure in folly for a last time wondering for a moment, if I'd really gone mad. As I searched the span, I know I saw a figure in white standing about mid-span watching me leave.

I know I saw a figure watching me leave. I am not mad.

The sail home was uneventful, no squalls, though there were thunderheads in the distance to the west. They were traveling northeast and would miss me. Not that thunderstorms frighten me; they don't, but when the sea whips up as you sail and gusts of wind keep you thinking every minute you haven't time to muse. It was gusty but I managed. I am glad it was not a fretful trip.

I kept reviewing in my mind what I had seen, and kept wondering why I hadn't seen it before. I couldn't pass it as an illusion, it was real, and the figure was of human shape and dimension that had no relativity to the bridge span or part of a construction. It was a human shape, it was in the bridge and I saw it. He was there.

I thought much about this folly of a day, alternately chastising myself for having given in to a notion, and reaffirming the notion I saw something in that span. How could I handle all this when I got back to Key West?

Undoubtedly I would be roundly censured for my selfishness, taking the boat for myself for the day. I reasoned: "why not, it's my boat, and if I wanted to be alone for a few hours, why not? Everyone wants his alone time on "occasion". Excuses for my seeming inconsiderateness, were mounting to where I felt I could excuse myself for any capital crime on the books. Suffice it to say to them, "I wanted some time off by myself." Then I heard, "That's OK too, but why couldn't you simply have said so instead of sneaking off like someone on a 'dark' mission?" "I didn't want to discuss it, that's why!" "Very well, then perhaps we can be as antisocial as you." Would this tart banter end it all? I knew not. Eventually it would have to be accepted; I would not begin to enlighten anyone about my trip or fantasies.

Over the years I have learned never, tell anyone about what I felt deep inside. As soon as you reveal something about yourself, about who you are, you immediately become vulnerable, and in the end of it, when your relationships break down, that moment becomes the heat and heart of the debate or used against you.

I remember, as a child, I revealed myself to others, and my revelations became topic to be discussed at cocktail parties. I learned never to reveal my dreams or talk about my fantasies; you will be judged by them.

Through my life, I have learned to expose little of myself and never to expose those things that are relevant to my souls' life. I do not think I am alone in this.

We all have our deepest thoughts and feelings we cannot share. If we do, it is only on the surface. The notion you will feel better if you open up is for the birds.

No one can flesh out your thoughts. Sometimes not even you can, because they are mercurial and in the peripheral. They don't bear the light of day, being simple flashes of self-insight, even you don't comprehend.

I knew from my experience I could not ever mention that I saw a man in a white suit waving at me in this bridge span. On the other hand, that there was something about the span of which I was a part, not even if I was aware of it, if that makes sense and it doesn't.

All this sailing down the Keys. Time was lost, having worn no watch, I couldn't know what time it was, the sun was surely over the yard-arm long ago, it being well past noon. It felt three o'clock give or take.

I was now hungry, and if my stomach was a judge of time, it was well past lunch. I went below to see if there were any provisions stowed away. There were supplies aboard, Ice in the icebox, beer, soda. How stupid, not checking first and allowing my hunger to come upon me, then finding here were things to eat and drink.

Was I becoming possessed with this? Was reality being pushed into receding echoes of my mind? Enough reality was there to sail the boat, or was that automatic?

In my dream, of what I had just done, all other realities of my life were shunted aside. I operated on automatic pilot. Now that the adventure, for lack of a better word, was terminating, all the things daily life pushes at you were coming to the fore. I had to relieve myself; I did with the satisfaction of peeing over the side. I chuckled, as I always do when I pee over the side, remembering a story my father told me about a trip he made with his father and uncles on one of their sailing yachts. He was about five, so it was about 1910. Anyway all the men peed over the side, my guess this was a 'gentlemen only sail' and he, and being a little boy, had to stand on the rail to pee, as he did, the boat lurched and he peed on himself. Of course, he was deeply chagrined because of his accident, but even more, because his father and his uncles all roared with laughter so did the crew. I learned. Never pee into the wind or when there are waves. I made a sandwich. It was as if someone knowing I would be away for a time had thoughtfully put ham, cheese, and mayonnaise and other victuals on board. Actually, I could have stayed away a couple of days. I was that well supplied. I knew there was ample butane to cook with, if I wanted. I was sure there was an answer why the boat was so well provisioned, I hadn't done it. Well never mind, that is how it was. Now I began to relax and enjoy the sail down, the day was not lost entirely.

When I pulled up to our dock and secured the boat for the night, I suddenly remembered we were originally supposed to take our guests out for a picnic. Ah-so, that's the reason for the full larder! Ah-not-so were the glares filled with reproach as I went into the house. There were towels and all the stuffs one would take on an outing. Thank God for the pool, was all I could think.

I did feel bad about letting these people down, but not so bad. I was abjectly apologetic about it. In situations like this, there is no simple explanation you can give. All you can do is tell people you are sorry.

I said, "I had an errand I wanted to take care of, and I quite simply forgot the day was for an outing until I was on my way back. I did not have my cell phone with me and there is no phone on board or any way I could be in contact with shore. Otherwise, I would have called you. If everyone wants to, we can do the sail tomorrow. Nothing is so lost it can't be replaced." My statement did little to mollify. I was not about to go into lot of labyrinthine explanations; the simpler the better.

Tell as much as you have to, to get out of hot water and be as close to the truth as you can, and in that, there are bits and pieces that hold up the rest of the story. Later I knew I would be pressed for some kind of larger explanation, but for now, what I said stood.

To sweeten the kitty of disappointment, I offered to take the party to the Palm for dinner. At their prices, I could certainly lard my guilt appropriately in the eyes of the disappointed. An expensive dinner can always make people happy with disappointment.

I excused myself and went into our bedroom to take a shower and have nap before we descended on the Palm, where   I had entreated the owner to make room in his Saturday night guest list.   Eight people were a bit much for him, but because he knew me and I ate there fairly frequently, he obliged.   Eight people with wine would be a big check.   He could make room for that.

I felt somewhat exonerated for my effort to provide an evening for people, who I liked well enough to share my house for a time with, but did not feel so taken with them, or in love or lust with any of them that I had to extend myself beyond good manners and warm feelings in general.   These, by and large were not my friends, but those of my better half.

Better halves, as the saying goes, have agendas and friends, not yours, but become yours because life is inclusive to the extent your interests in relationships are dual so long as it affects your being together. This was one of those times.

We had guests, three couples.   In today's world they were not odd; two men, two women, and a man and a woman.   We had room for them all, two guest rooms with baths and an enclosed gazebo we used in emergencies. To be absolutely fair, they drew lots to see who would be put up or out and have to share a bath.

Luckily, the downstairs bathroom opens onto the terrace by the pool. There wasn't too much discomfort for any one. I love to sleep in the gazebo.   It has two large benches with comfortable cushions that make up into beds, lots of pillows and a large coffee table and chairs.

I suppose the so-called discomfort would be in guest storage, which is located in the house near the guest powder room. There is a huge walk-in closet with a chest, full-length mirror and all the creature comforts except to be next door to where you are sleeping.

The gazebo is really quite gala and the sides shutter to create absolute privacy. I wouldn't give up my room to be in there, but I do like it better than the guest rooms. Everything is air conditioned, but we never use it, even on the hottest days. The house opens up nicely. The roof opens and the doors fronting the terrace and the pool so the entire area is a flowing space. The lot is a double lot so there is lots of garden.

The man who built the house has remarkable taste and a sure feel what is style without pretense. He put in instant jungle and we are screened from everything going on outside the gate. If you wanted to, you could run around stark naked and no one would know the difference.

I showered and took a nap. I dreamed. I was at the bridge. This time I tied the boat to something, it being a dream; made perfect sense.

I climbed into the span and looked about. There was nothing to see. Dappled sun, moving water casting shadow, but nothing that did not have the rhythm of natural being. It, being a dream, my awake mind kept telling me this, and my sub-conscious; really? Telling me, I was suspended in suspension. I was beyond reality. My reality of this moment held me, part here part there; then through the fragmented, the shadows a figure moved in contrast to the surrounding movement.

There was the man.

It, being a dream, I knew he wasn't more than a figment of my last glance at the bridge. What more could I know than that?

In my dreams, I had many times imagined people I had never known or seen. They were drawn from other things; composites, perhaps of people I had seen. My dreams largely focused on events that had nothing to do with my daily life. Although sometimes daily life intruded to a point. This being a dream the whole thing had plot beyond time.

I have that faculty of closing my eyes and dreams come in a second of my going into slumber. My conscious mind, always at work, gives in to my dream with reluctance, so I enjoy them in tandem.

I dreamt I was in the bridge. The man was there, in the bridge. It being a dream, there was no caution between us. We smiled as old friends meeting would. It being a dream, we embraced, as you would greet someone you knew all your life, but hadn't seen for years. Strange, I thought he is clean-shaven as I am. Of course, intruded my conscious mind; this is a dream.

We sat in one of the girders, our legs dangling over the water. The boat below was bobbing about. We laughed at its maneuvers "Did you have a good trip up?" "Oh not eventful in the least, shot up easily, good breeze." "I know, I watched for your coming". "You did? How did you know?" "You told me you'd be back in your dream."

I wondered how I became a part of all this, and why; what in my life, apart from all its daily exigencies made me come here? We all escape at times from our daily lives. Even the driven take time from the plod. Then, being driven go back to being driven.

Now and then, ephemera catch our side-glance and we follow it, charmed at its being there for us to see. We become chasers of butterflies or whatever shape ephemera come in, for us. We are led down the path of fantasy for a moment before we catch ourselves up and waken from the dream in reality-to-reality and the ephemera, whether it was a person far from our ken, or experience beyond anything we would normally do.

It takes so many shapes and the experience is solely ours to have. In my life, this sort of thing is rooted in sex, I guess for most people it is rooted in sex.

Sex is a creature in fantasy knows no bounds; in reality is rooted in the moment. To translate it from vision to flesh takes a lot of work; we may have to give up so much. To be stroked and kissed in one's dreams is totally different than when one has to pander to a partner's dream. It is all these levels to cope with.

A fantasy, dream or not, you have it all your way, and if you really work at it you can have all the sensation of lovemaking. How often have you wakened from a particularly sensuous dream to find yourself very much wanting to go right back to sleep to see if there is a moment more, like a last drop?

We are always making love with our dream. For a time in our lives, we make love with our better half or someone on the side. It is rarely something approaching fantasy. Even in its reality, we dwell in fantasy to help us through. It's a terrible thing to say about your partner; but consider, your partner is probably in the same boat. I have found very few people end up with the person who best represents their ideal. Getting along is what it is all about; mundane to say the least. Then to dream, you can't be chastised for your dreams.

We sat on the girder watching the sea. Our backs were away from US-One with its bustle of cars. We heard nothing. Coming toward us was a fishing boat with people in it, a pleasure ride, no one was fishing. I couldn't tell if they saw us sitting there or not. They made no salute as they approached.

I said to the man who lived in the trestle bridge; "that's funny, they did not wave to us or acknowledge our presence." "They cannot see us." "They can't see the boat?" I asked, "No, we are not here to them." I looked startled, he continued. "We are lost in light and shadow; they are busy in their own worlds." "And we?" I asked "And we are busy in ours."

Then he said in a familiar voice, "It is getting near time for us to leave, wake up." In that flash he was gone and I sat bolt upright to see dusk outside and all the lights on the deck lit and the pool lighted too.

The master bedroom is off the deck and opens directly to the outside. I looked out, the room was dark, and so no one saw me in the nude peering out at them. "Come on, it's getting late, we've already started drinks." Out the door, breezing away at everyone went my dream crasher dammed awakener.

I crossly got up and put on some shorts and a pullover shirt. The crowd, for lack of a better word, was in high spirits. When I made my entrance, all seemed forgiven for their lack of a day aboard the boat. They were anticipating a really good meal at the Palm, rather than a home cooked one here.

I entered, as best I could, into the spirit of the thing, having a Scotch and soda and some canapé. Talk swirled around me and did not really include me because it was about their lives. These were not my friends, come to think of it, I had no friends of my own. It has never really occurred to me that I had no friends of my own. We have been together so long that companions became ours rather than ones or the others. Our friends were the result of building social relationships beginning with invitations from us both, but decided upon without much input from me.

I went along for the ride. My business life had its acquaintances, but not social responsibilities other than lunch or dinner at a public place in gala situations. Come to think of it, I was reticent about bringing others into our social network. It was too much responsibility to meld diverse personalities in such a way as to make or create a coterie of friends.

Our guests were 'New Yorker' types, full of themselves, up on everything, chatty, effusive full of plans and possibilities for their lives. My other half was more their milieu, and, indeed, was chirpy as they were. They were all in the same madness, career-wise, they all knew the same people, gossiped about every one.

I suddenly wondered why they ever missed me; I was not one bit of their world. Outside of providing company and nice 'digs', restaurant food and a boat to sail in, who was I in all this? Maybe I was invisible, as I was in the dream. I paid for my boat trip with a dinner check in excess of $700. It is amazing how much wine it takes to mollify hurt feelings.

They all decided to do the bars and discos.   I begged off pleading a hard day at the helm. I was let off from further revels with ease. Perhaps I had been a bit of a churl when I refused to order wine with the high recommendation of the sommelier at $50 a bottle. $25 for an unspoiled California was quite enough, and did its job. No sense getting drunk at $50 a bottle when $25 will do the same trick. It's all in the price, you see; $50 is smoother going down and $25 clings to the palette, so they say. After the first swallow it all feels or swallows the same, especially on top of scotch and gin and food.

Anyway, let off the hook, as I was, I ambled home through the back streets, a long amble, and in Key West, the back streets are a contradiction in so many ways.   Next to a Conch house, run down with a derelict car out front, might be a spanking white cottage or remodeled Key West two-story Victorian manse, white fence and all. Interesting contrast, rather like life, in a way.

You spend life observing contrasts; on the one hand you see beggars on the street calling for a hand outs, and men and women nattily dressed walking by them in disgust, usually observing they wouldn't be hungry if they had a job. We presume from appearances the natty people have money and jobs. Maybe they don't at all. They may be living on the edge of ruin in style, their next move bringing them into the beggar's realm.   Beggars have no money, or they wouldn't beg, except begging has become a profession paying rather well.

Dependent on your point of view, begging is an antisocial occupation, like drug dealing, except a drug dealer can make a lot of money, and that is what it is all about isn't it?   Our obsession with money no matter how it is got is what runs society.

The most outrageous people get into society from any point of projection.   One need have no more talent than exposure of the moment. There is so much space to fill in every medium of communication, and having to fill it makes the bizarre commonplace to the lowest common denominator and all realize they too can partake if they have a gimmick. For however fleeting the spotlight shines on them, it is satisfactory. And we, unfortunate voyeurs, lap it like cream because it extends our lives.

It is easy to have thoughts like these in Key West walking along darkened streets. In another place I might not feel safe, the times being what they are. I am not all that sanguine about this, but somehow I feel fate is watching my star, as it were, and I'll be quite alright.

The night is warm, about 79 degrees, comfortable for walking, sleeping, making love without covers, or with covers for that matter. Making love under any circumstances is pretty spectacular.

I am perfectly sure by the time every one returns home there will be none of that; it will be too late and too much will have been drunk to make it probable. The possibility is all mine. No it won't be tonight, nor will it be tomorrow night. Tomorrow night everyone will be a flurry to pack to catch the plane north.

I have the luxury of a few more days, actually, truth be told, for as long as it pleases me. There is no hubbub waiting at the other end. The luxury of being alone in a somewhat peaceful time is something to look forward to; I can examine my navel.

At the risk of seeming mean, and perhaps I am, I will wake everyone bright and early and give them the sail they missed yesterday.

I am sure they will arrive home and will entertain hangovers in the morning. A good brisk sail will brighten that crew.

The night sky is clear as a bell and the moon is on the rise. It is so bright it blurs the stars, except for a planet or two. I can't remember if it is Jupiter or Venus or Mars who is out tonight. A sailor would have a hard time with celestial navigation on a night like this. Tomorrow will be one of those advertisers write about.

It's about 8:00 A. M. now; the French Bakery on Duval Street is open for breakfast. I'll ride my bike up to get some Croissants and rolls and a baguette. If the pastries look good, well, why not show my generous side. Got back, no one is up, now 8:30. Squeezed orange juice, made coffee, set the table. Had everything except the New York Times.

It's amazing, you get away from all the hustle of you life at home to escape the news, and the first thing you miss is the Times.

The Miami Herald is an absolute shambles. A cretin would find it fascinating. I'm sure they do. You never have to worry about where to buy an automobile or plumbing supplies. If advertising makes a paper solvent, then the Miami Herald must wallow in thunder bucks. I guess that is why a semi-literate like me gets the Times; at least there is a rise in my ability to comprehend what is going on. (Even the Times has succumbed to shoddy editing and workmanship in presentation, spelling errors all over the place, and grammar, for the lack of a better word, is outward bound taking the English language to a murky graveyard.) Being literate is almost as bad as being a virgin at the age of 20; on the one hand no one understands you and on the other one wonders what went wrong. Both perplex.

8:45: everybody up! It's a gorgeous day, great day for a sail, hurry up now, move it out! Coffee, fresh orange juice and fresh croissants for everybody! I went banging around in a positively sadistic manner; after all, I had an audience of masochists to warm to.

After all, getting in at 4:00 AM, full of ribaldry and giggles until after 5:00, awakening me with buff dips in the pool, splashing all about, now they had to pay; Aha!

What a disappointment. They chirped up a storm happily, though sleepily anticipating the days sail. Were they not hung over? How indecent of them!

Was it my perception people who stay out until all hours are, of necessity, hung-over the next day? Well if they were, they masked it much to my disgust. No reason to be sadistic unless it pays.

It's amazing what fresh orange juice, fresh coffee, and fresh croissants will do for people in fresh air and sunshine after a dip in the pool. How can some people positively bubble like freshly opened Champagne having debauched all night, it is disgusting! Even my better half was in good spirits, though on a few hours sleep cheerfulness is not her outstanding virtue.

Off we went, swim suits, shorts, towels, suntan lotion, a plethora of absolute necessities and some more food. The refrigerator aboard had managed to keep everything fresh since yesterday. Even so, they must have thought I consumed quantities. Oh well.

We sailed into the Atlantic. The breeze picked up and we were off to the south, away from the trestle bridge. We sailed through to the Caribbean because I didn't want to in any way be tempted to sail north.

That bridge was mine, not to share. One thing about private adventure is sure; if you even hint of it, even to your cat, someone else will demand to know what you are up to; they want to share. Blech to sharing! It's mine and I want to keep it mine. Soon enough I could go and once again explore the outer reaches.

We sailed leisurely around the muffin islands, exploring here and there, dropping anchor to splash in the water. It was shallow and I had to sail carefully not to go aground. We picnicked on all sorts of goodies and the mood was generally jolly. Imminent knowledge vacation was nearly over cast a slight pall on the group fest.
The remarkable thing about this place called the Keys is: no matter who you are, you are pulled into your own safe haven, recognizing more and more who you are and putting off as long as long as possible getting back to real life. Even the people who service the Keys stay because the place offers shelter from an abusive world in their free time. They work to stay.

Personalities change to a calmer demeanor. All this may be hogwash in reality. I'm sure the same anti-social behavior abounds as it does elsewhere, but the difference is, it is different, hard to explain. You have to live it for a while before you understand. It is a small town with the same gossipy air other small towns thrive on. A day in a boat among muffin islets takes away all the feeling of being trapped in a larger world. Each person is his own islet, free to join without the implication of other beings so enjoined.

There was much rehash of the ten days spent together, most of it congenial, some seemingly pre-PMS in attitude, but for the most part frosted over recognizing we are all subject to moods. There was plenty of space to be alone beaches to burn on, waters to swim, by evening tempers tempered themselves to hospitable attitudes.

Grouse as I may, and I do, they all pitched in and did enormous shares of house keeping, cooking, dishes, pool cleaning and gardening. They made considerable contributions to the larder and the wine cellar without stinginess or being pressured into being good guests.

Our house rule is: this is your room, if you make the bed, you do, if it's a mess; it's yours to live with while you are here. We do not do housework any more than necessary.

It is a rule that seems to work. Not having been a houseguest often, I forget people are genuinely grateful for the getaway. You forget gratitude, unfortunately, unless you experience grace often.

It was a charming day. All of us in the company and each of us in our occasional reveries. We packed it in and sailed to civilization about three-thirty. It was nearly five when we reached shore. We spent another half hour putting the boat to 'sleep' for the night.

Everyone was hot to see one more sunset from the roof of the Holiday Inn. After showers and swims we trudged off to the Holiday Inn's always welcoming roof.

There were people aplenty, and looking west was a cruise ship beginning to blink lights on. As usual, the sunset was brilliant and everyone cheered when the last rays spilled over the surface of the sea sending light shafts afloat in darkening waves. I must have seen the sunset a hundred times or more. People who have visited have had to go to the Holiday Inn roof, and of course, I had to go too. You would think, old crud that I am, I'd seen it enough. Not at all, it amazes me every time. No two are alike in all the time in existence. No two alike. I'll stick by that one.

We spent a quiet, somewhat reflective evening, over a long dinner wanting to postpone the inevitable for as long as possible. When you go to bed the last evening you are away, you subconsciously gear up for the next day's next travel, either dashing to the airport or going leisurely, depending on how things move in the morning. The clock ticks unmercifully from good night to good bye.

Talking, musing as one and all are wont to do. You find depth in people you hadn't realized was there. It is all in talk, people reaching into their souls to reflect what depth there is in, I guess, everyone.

You always have to catch that mood, that moment hung in time where you are not challenged by all the forces that drive you day by day. It is then you can bare your innermost thoughts because you are safe from challenge of what you feel.

What we believe is different from what we feel because it is stated as a creed and is far flung from what we permit ourselves to look at. Belief is that thing we are taught by rote, the tenet driven into our conscious mind. Feeling is accepting doubt our beliefs are all that well built. To question is to doubt, and we are not given that right.

Amazing little things occupy our feelings, simple wishes, and simple pleasures finally. These were things we talked about. Stripped away from the veneer we stalk our lives with is simplicity we only dream is ours.

This place permits everyone who will, to strip away the pompisities of life. Most assuredly there are tourists who never lose it and wonder where the magic is. For them it never will be because the load they carry is never allowed to be lifted long enough to absorb what lives really are.

I listened to these people talk and I wondered why I hadn't a clue who they were. My supposition is; they were as afraid of me as I of them. They were on holiday away from the fractious lives they daily led. I found myself with sadness knowing they would be gone along with the moment this was. Had they stayed longer, would this be continuance at another dinner? Would the charade be played deftly as it had been these past ten days? I will never know, nor will they, or were this evening's reflections on the value of life to be passed by as the hours?

The inevitable dawn came with thinking about thunderheads to the west. We will probably have a shower or two today. Everyone went quietly about their business, looking around for some misplaced item, packing last minute bits and pieces, getting dressed in gear that bespoke city life and the panache look of returning rested vacationers.

All this show through airports into taxis and to final destinations to a doorman opening the cab door remarking about the tan. That is worth an extra dollar. For some getting out of the subway standing with gear in hand, looking tan, and watching riders, looking grey, envying you. It ends with your putting a key in a lock and walking in to a private little place you remember.

Last night had been what I thought; no love making. Well it was late by the time the dishes were put into the dishwasher and the dining area was cleaned of major debris. I am one of those people who will not go to bed knowing there is mayhem to waken to in the kitchen in the morning. Of course, by the time I got to bed, my companion in life was asleep. You can always tell when your lover, be it wife or husband, is avoiding contact in bed. The body lies on its side away from you so that contact cannot be accidental. The body is stiff and breathing very quiet, not one iota of relaxation or invitation. You or they recognize the animal from an atavistic point, which says, 'don't touch, not tonight'. In theory, it would only be days before I had to leave paradise, so perhaps then.

Goodbye, yes we had a wonderful time...come back soon, when you can stay longer and the rest of the departure litany on both sides. A bread and butter note in verbiage. Of course, the real thing will follow directly. We too, said a fond goodbye, my being given a gentle remonstration for my seeming unfathomable behavior the last few days.

I protested, of course, feeling, at times, hemmed in by all the frenetic activity. It allowed so little time for us. I was assured we had a lot of time together, and all that 'stuff' would be taken care of. Making love, 'stuff?' like laundry, to be handled? It is not quite like brushing your teeth!

The drive from the airport is along the beach whether you drive north or south. Going north you round the Key and have a choice of going down the shopping and tourist way. I waited until the plane was safely off and had flown off into the 'blue yonder' which a fluff of thunderheads, so innocent was looking. I was now on my own, without constraints except my own.

There wasn't much traffic going north; there was coming south and I made a mental note there could be slowdowns, especially as you drove from Key to Key.

I drove to the vegetable stand I go to and picked up a few things from the fellow who owns the place. He lives there with his wife and children surrounded by boxes, crates a run down truck parked as near to the highway as the law allows. The side of the truck proclaims fresh fruit and vegetables. Sometimes there is an American flag stuck in at a rakish angle to lure, or at least get people to reflect the vision in their minds and come off the road to buy some vegetables.

He had great oranges and grapefruit today, so I bought a lot, also some bananas, limes and zucchini and mushrooms and onions. As I aimlessly picked first one then another and yet more, it flicked across my mind why? I am alone, expecting no one, well maybe I'd have my pal in for dinner, but that was it. Here I was buying as if I had planned to stay beyond my days committed. Subconsciously I must've known I was not hurrying back.

I meandered back to the house, arriving to see all the disarray left by the departed. It was threatening rain so I decided not to go for a sail, but to round up sheets and towels and launder. The guest room clean up could wait until the cleaners from the realtors came by to get the house ready for future renters. (One thing: if you own a house in not only Key West, but say London, New York, or any place where there is tourist traffic, it pays to have the house available for travelers who want a place, not a hotel, for a period, which approximates a home. Generally, it pays the taxes and upkeep so you live free.)

Our house is in good demand, so I cannot be too cavalier about how much time I take without prior notice to the realtors. However, the house was not booked for another month, it being between seasons. Regardless, there was pool service, and if I wanted, cleaning. Sheets and towels are a manor chore. I did keep the bedroom and bath in reasonable shape as well as the living, dining room, and kitchen. I have a few friends in Key West, people who live and make a living here, and from time to time I entertain them.

One of them is our realtor. She specializes in rental properties, hence, the management of mine. She is a transplant to Key West and can't imagine living anywhere else. She knows most of the gossip, which in Key West hardly goes beyond who is sleeping with whom, or who has a new boat, a baby, a house; nothing acrimoniously scandalous that I would be told about anyway. I decided to have her over to dinner for a quiet evening. The showers blew away and it was clear and sparkling, warm and balmy.

We were having a drink by the pool. The air was delicious, some Jasmine was in bloom, and perfumed the surroundings. The lights were on in the garden, highlighting the Bougainvillea in blossom climbing the house, terrible stuff, but pretty.

The banana frond was producing a nice bunch of bananas in the near future and the lime tree was dropping limes. And yes the grapefruit tree, why did I buy them when I could sell them, same with the limes. You forget the riches of your own back yard just sitting there for the asking. Ah well, such is life, sit on a gold mine and dig for tin. Anyway, we were talking in general terms about this and that, nothing specific, confidences are given sparingly, as they always are.

You can spend hours engaged discussing the deepest philosophy with a person you know but never know a single thing about that person. Sometimes I think it even goes into relationships. You can live with someone for years and never know who he or she is. You get glimpses of the deeper person, but rarely more than that. All we are is facade to be judged on by what is seen. We agreed life is a riddle. Alternatively, it is very simple because we are complex, and decorate it with convolution to meet our demands and fantasies.

We dined on roast chicken; no finer fare than that. We became laconic with wine, musing at nothing and ventured into near silence.

I broke the reverie asking when she last driven above Marathon. You have to remember most Key Westers are loathe to leave except on some errand needing presence. If they go off island, it is on a plane to Miami or New York. To drive north of Cudjoe Key is a trip.

She said it had not been too long a time. A long time meant within six months. I asked her if she'd ever noticed the trestle bridge. She allowed everyone noticed it. It stands alone being a sentinel to the past, like a monument. OK, that was obvious, and I knew in the Hurricane of Nineteen-thirty-five thousands perished all through the Keys. She said the bridge was believed to be haunted, but of course, it was not. So far as anyone knew, there was no one in the bridge, and if there were they perished.

People say they see things in the bridge. It is the light. It does funny things to the imagination. As she went on my mind was flummoxed. I must be imagining things. Did she ever see anything in the bridge, I asked. "I don't even think about it" she told me, "actually I am so happy to see that long stretch of nothing but white ribboned road ahead of me, and if the weather is good; there is nothing like the view."

Well that does it, I thought. I am going to put it out of my mind, maybe. It wads getting on, dinner had been eaten, coffee and brandy had by the pool, and as I mused, I saw reflections in the lighted pool, shadows of the trees, and thought maybe my friend was right; light plays tricks. Tied to imagination light can carry you outward toward other worlds.It was done then, my trip into the fantasy of The Trestle Bridge, light, clouds. Wishful thinking left me to the exploration of my mind as I drifted off to sleep.

Once again, we were sitting in the girders of the bridge. I was well aware it was a dream. Subconsciously it was an exploration into nether worlds. I was wary exposing myself, to perhaps, over entertainment of my psyche, but it led me on with the prospect of getting through the point of excursion.

o..o.oo..o..."I wondered if you would return," he said rather sadly. I caught the note in his voice and glanced sideways to see his expression. It was far away and sadness was, I felt, simply tethered loneliness there by himself. He continued, "I sent you messages and you seemed reluctant to acknowledge them in any way. I felt you were really going to reject the notion, I could be here, especially tonight when you were faced with another person's notion it was all fabrication of a mind." "Well isn't it," I answered, "This is a dream." He said, "return to the bridge and see for yourself." "How can I do that, I have to leave, and it may not be sailing weather again." "You can leave when you want; both of us know that, but do as you wish. Say so and I won't come to you in your dreams again." "What do you want me to do?" I asked, "What you please" was his answer. "Should I come to the bridge? Will you be there?" "You won't know unless you sail up, will you." With that, he faded away. He had never been in the bridge, but in the room, it seemed. The dream began in the girder, but ended in my bedroom. I awoke, and for the first time in years, recorded what I'd dreamt. Ordinarily I am not given to flights of fancy or dreams, but when a dream captures your mind to the extent you must heed its presence in your waked consciousness, you, however unwillingly, pay it attention.

This was not a fragment of something larger. This was the larger. It was as if I were being warned. Well at least apprised of something about to happen in my life. Like death? It did not feel threatening as death, of course dependent how you feel about dying. Somewhere along the line of my life I came to accept death as part of the process of existence and continuum. I was not fearful of the process of existence. It is, as all unknowns are, fraught with turning corners or walking through an unknown passageway to another scene in your life, not unlike those boat rides you took in an amusement park that led you from one panorama to another with extravagant scenes from history or literature. Undoubtedly, these panoramas were taken from high extreme to entertain.

In my childhood, they were stationery and as you passed and continued, their beady eyes stared out. The figures were in dramatic poses struck there as you passed and seemed to continue in movement after you left. Did these people never sleep? I understand some, for lack of a better word, amusement parks have these very things in full animation, which interact with the audience extracting reactions calculated to scare or amuse you. So much for your imagination being given a chance to preclude what was really going on. If you think of it, panorama is part of all our lives, and visited places we see, as they are; distant.

The next day was a 'galumphy' day. It hung there uninviting. Of course, it was not the day's fault, but him who lived it did it disservice. To wit, I was in a 'mood'. There had been a chirpy hello from the north, urging me return soon as I was missed. Oh sure, no love making, and I was missed? Humph! The weather was fine north, and everybody had a good time, of course they did, they were with me!

I believe in the vernacular it is called being brought up to speed. All well and good. The house stood. The apartment had not been disturbed. The car started. The maid had been there. The lawn mowed. On and on the litany sped on all of the things that did and did not happen during the ten days we were away, or that could have or not happened. My goodness, life's lot has been satisfactory. All that and heaven too did not change the overall picture of my mood. I was wrestling within my dreams and fantasies. Should I chuck the whole thing and get a plane out, or should I simply let the mood get on with itself and ebb as moods do.

Getting outside, even of one's self to the out of doors can change perspective. It was, of course, 'soft weather' shining and breezy. I'll trot over to get some croissant, or why not have breakfast, and get the Times, do the puzzle. Was it a hard day or an easy day, sadistic bum, that editor, clues too cute for words, and then the awful puns! Well, come on, let's go and take the challenge.

Actually, as I made my way I brightened. Why hurry back to New York when there is weather like this in Key West. Even if New York were gorgeous, life in the city is too busy even if you are not. There is always something to be done, keep up with, something nags away the day and keeps you alert to the pitfalls of standing still. Your eye is always catching some scene from the slice of life and beckoning you to assimilate yourself to it, even vicariously. Unless you are in your apartment, you are continually bombarded with intrusion of events as they unfold and something is always unfolding. No matter what activity you are engaged in, you are constantly being swept in your attention span to other complications, which, duly registered on your psyche to become part of the mirror of your life.

Where I am now, I amble down the street, or ride my bicycle. No one projects drama for my psyche to record and remember, even in my darkest brain.

One of the enumerable island cats caught up with me and pretended deepest affection hoping, I guess, that I could whip out some food for it to eat. Of course, I had none, but stopped to give her ear a scratch. She responded by arching her back and entwining herself in my legs. 'Sorry cat, I have nothing to feed you, not handy, anyway'. Here I presumed the cat was a 'she'. She was, but I presumed. Are females more affectionate? Female cats' maybe, but the female human species are another tale to tell. Anyway, Griselda, instant name, followed me, I guess to give me companionship.

Animals are so simple in extending their loyalty. The cat followed me, meandering along as I walked to get the newspaper, where she waited outside and then we walked down to the restaurant, which is an out of doors place in a garden. It was not overly busy and I got a nice big table off in a corner. No one noticed the cat followed me in. She sat at my feet just as if she belonged, which I guess by this time she did. I ordered, and the waiter brought coffee and little containers of cream. He must have thought I was somewhat mad. I opened all of them and poured them in the dish they came in, and put the dish down on the floor. The cat, of course, lapped it all up, content. When she finished I picked the dish and put all the little empty containers back in the dish. I drank my coffee black. I sat there reading about all the ghastly things that were happening in the world and wondered; why? Morbid curiosity, perhaps. Reading about things you cannot stop, things you cannot feel, yes, you are aware, but it seems to me the human race no longer feels anything. We are becoming devoid of being able to see how we are reflected.

We walked back to the house as if we had been steady companions for a long time. Cats, independent souls, to the untrained eye are totally dependent on a measure of interactive love from us. Their motto bravo; 'when in doubt, wash' was and is a ploy to gain time to see how the land lies. They are ever ready to jump away in a moment's glance or glare, or at the moment, smiled on, will smile back and urge you to know; you are noticed. I love cats, and dogs and animals in general. I guess if I were on intimate terms with a tiger I could love one without reservation. I have never understood cruelty to animals, and get incensed when I hear of or know of a dog or cat or any living creature being abused. Children who are badly treated by others make me cry and rage at the abuser. How could anyone kill a baby for crying from hunger, or a child paralyzed with fright? That is what I mean when I say society cannot look in a mirror and see itself as it is. We are all reflected in those images. We have become that monster we see in others. We pray to make them better. When it is also in us to be better.

I felt myself becoming obsessed with thoughts that were removed from the moment. I bent down and the cat came to me for a scratch on the ear. She was all smiles. She had seduced me. What would I do with her when it became time to leave? I was projecting too far into the future. I was not leaving today and tomorrow would take care of itself.

I opened the gate to the garden and 'Miss Galivantress' pranced right in as though she had done this a thousand times before. Maybe she had, maybe she lived in my house when I was not there. Perhaps when the place was rented she hung about determining whether or not the renters were 'cat' people. If they were; she was an amusement to them and they fed and adored or whatever cat people do. When no one was about perhaps, she simply lived in the gazebo and ate mice or other things cats eat. She made herself at home. I like to think she felt she was at home because she was home.

We spent the day lounging and snoozing, reading the Times, doing the puzzle; what a lulu it was, but we did get through it. About mid-afternoon, I thought to go down to the boat and bring in towels or any food we missed, and just look around. Madame La Chat ambled on with me to the dock and cast a wary eye at the boat, not sure, if this was within her bailiwick to explore. I opened the hatch and checked the fridge, and all the other things one does and saw nothing was left undone. We had done a good job on Sunday of cleaning up and cleaning out. Oh well, nothing to scrub so I sat on the cushion on the aft deck just to feel the gentle slap of the water hitting the side of the boat.

It was a rocking feeling that made me drowsy, the sun was waning. The cat assumed I guess that the place I was not harmful to cats and jumped aboard and carefully made her way to where I was. We just sat there, cat and pet.

She lay on the pad next to me and nestled close. I put my hand down to hold her and when I was settled she put her head on my hand just as if we belonged. The water slapped rhythmically and the boat rocked gently and we dozed and dreamed. She dreamed before I dozed because I felt her twitch as if involved in an adventure, and I drifted off.

Once again, I dreamt we were at sea, as they say in the crosswords. The cat sat on the hatch looking intently at all there was about her. She did not even seem tenuous but alert. I sat where I had been sitting and in my waking dream wondered how all this happened. It was late morning, the boat was moving right along at quite a clip, and of course, north toward the bridge, this was after all, a dream. In the shadow of reality, there is surrealism, and in the middle place is where nothing makes sense, being of two worlds.

His voice came in on the wind and greeted me. "How do you like your companion?" I answered, not the least bit startled, "You mean Missy La Chat?" "Yes, I thought she'd be a pleasant diversion for you." "But what will I do with her when I go home?" "Home? Really? I thought you were at home here." "I can be at home anywhere, what it takes is finding yourself in a place, and finding a comfort there. For me it can be anywhere." "Even in a trestle bridge?" "Well it does stretch the imagination to a great degree." "How about with a cat?" The thought of spending my life in a trestle bridge even with a cat rather stretches the imagination further than me.

Spending the rest of my life in a trestle bridge, how? The thought seemed, at best, ungainly; unmanageable at least, and most lacking creature comforts. And what are creature comforts? Indoors? It's a start. It does protect you from elemental forces. We build from there. The cave was the first room. We have expanded our horizons ever since. Simple enough to carry through to personal preference. Spend my life in a trestle bridge? As what? Would I be a figment from the fourth dimension? In a dream you are three-dimensional self is moot: you are fourth dimension.

"What would I do on the trestle bridge for the rest of my life?" I asked my friend. "What do you fancy doing?" he asked. "It's a little difficult to imagine, sitting on a girder looking out over the horizon, and hiding from intruders. The fun in that is limited". "Stretch! For goodness sake stretch your mind out of your dreams into the reality of existence." "What do you mean by that?" "Why must you be earth bound? Does it never enter your mind to be high flown?" "My mind is ever inquisitive, it knows no bounds." "Apparently it does. You presume yourself in a physical trestle bridge, unattached at either end. You will not imagine you are that trestle bridge, unattached providing crossing for nothing, standing as a monument to a dream. It is a metaphor, as you are." "I am a metaphor?" "Yes aren't we all? We are unattached at either end of our lives and the bridge we build stands alone for the possibility others will look at us as we them, and have momentary investigations who we are, perhaps to stay awhile in the girders of our lives. We are all a metaphor in existence in all its factors. You look askance at the notion of being what all creation is; stuck in time, which does not exist except as the hours are struck."

"What am I then? What are we all? What is the universe?" "Quite simply, as you are, as is all you know or imagine you know, shape given to the pulse of existence, which has no shape, but gives shape to all who would imagine it, and to all creation to the furthest star burning bright to heat its satellites into being to create what can be imagined." "And that is life and death?" "There is neither, it is all simply being in continuum to what ever form you choose to be at that moment."

"Then who are you?" "I am you in a different form" "You are me?" "...to the extent we are each other where we are. We are each other in existence, whatever form we take. We are alike because that is what shape is devised this moment for you to be. Elsewhere you might be something else." "A rock? A stick?" "No, you are given specific life, in other realms in this form. You may be primitive. In some places, you might even be me. Think about it." With that he was gone.

Madame La Chat was still nestled in the crook of my arm, seemingly unaware what I had just been through. I glanced about me to see if I was where I had been; and I was. Rather than disturb the sleeping cat, I lay there wondering about all this. There was definitely something working its way into my consciousness to realize. Could I recall all I dreamt, or would I forget and reconstruct pieces of it that were convenient to my memory? Regardless, I could capture the essence of the thought and begin to understand something of what was being projected into my brain and, for lack of a better term; soul consciousness. Those words had other connotations in this day and age and were not specifically part of my vocabulary dealing with things in my everyday life. What, then, was going on?

The Madame stirred, stretched and blinked a look about, not being assured she was where she should be, and as cats are wont to do, she immediately began to wash her face. As she moved, it allowed me to sit up and try to fathom what time it was. I had no watch on. I never wear one in Key West. I arrive and shed all my city affectations as quick as I can. Right offhand I couldn't remember what time I came aboard, ah yes, mid-afternoon. How long had I been asleep? The sun wasn't particularly setting, so it must be fiveish. Was I hungry? Not particularly. Did I want a drink of water? Scotch? Not particularly. I roused myself, stood and stretched and sat down again. I worked my mind back to my dream. There seemed to be answers, but what were the questions? The whole prospect was daunting. I seemed to have in my grasp answers to riddles not posed. Now I had answers. I have to contemplate questions to fit those not asked.

I stood again, and this time, put things in shipshape order, closing the hatch and locking it, and then checked the lines to make sure we were secure. Madame followed me approving every move. We left the boat and walked up the dock and back to the house.

The sun set again. I sat by the pool absorbing the encroaching darkness. About a million miles away at the Holiday Inn and on the pier tourists were applauding the fact the sun was setting on another day. I sat by the pool.

I spent some time in reverie, the outside lights came on. Garden and pool were bathed in light with a blink, just like that. The house remained dark; I had to turn those lights on. Some hours later the lights would all go out, and once again, the garden and the pool would be dark, much like life.

Is life like the sunrise and sunset; a light turning on then off again and again? Are we trestle bridges that stand as enduring monuments? Trestle bridges erode if left to their devices and nature, and finally become absorbed into the matter around them. Are we like that?

Is the ritual of burial a return to the elements, ashes to ashes, dust to dust? It must be, because it has long been the hope of man to return to what creation made him.

It is the undertaker who embalms to preserve, and sells you a casket guaranteed not even to crumble in time, then places you in a mausoleum to make sure no element touches you to harm your dead body. One prays your spirit has long flown to escape such entrapment. I have always thought being wrapped in a sheet and put in a hole below the frost line was the best.

I never thought much about cremation. In India, it is quite the way to go. I cannot see how they have a Sandalwood tree left, not any tree left, for that matter.

It makes me remember when my father died. I went to the undertaker, who immediately showed me a line of caskets ranging from two-thousand to five thousand Dollars. I had told him the old boy was to be cremated, and asked incredulously; "do you mean you burn the casket too?" He unctuously told me, it too was for the fire. What a waste! He showed me a walnut job, walnut, yet, with bronze handles; this was going to be burned? "What happens to the handles" I asked. "Oh, they melt down." I thought something like "give me a break!" Finally, we got down to "utility." It was a two-hundred Dollar job lined with rayon satin instead of silk.

The undertaker sniffed it certainly would not look good in Church. Well it did; the Church had a blanket, that and a bunch of roses made the whole thing look great. No one ever knew whether the casket was wood or what.

 Here is an amusement; the undertaker asked me what clothes Papa would wear to eternity. Not being sure the soul would be clothed or naked, believe me, I am aware, this is the body, and the soul is what it is, and no soul goes on to whatever wearing clothes, at least not as we know them. To be sure, one never knows, I mean, one could stand there stark naked in front of all the recently dead. All of whom would be decked out, and there you would be, naked as a jaybird. Of course, all those people killed in war, babies, children would be there too in whatever they were or were not wearing when they were buried or burned. Do you suppose you meet these souls as ash if they were cremated? Not to digress too far; I got a natty sports jacket, shirt, tie, trousers, underwear, and his favorite hat. I was going to make sure he was going to   arrive wherever he was going in style.

I do not think I believed all this, but I was not going to fly in the face of tradition. It was a closed casket, so I never knew if he was dressed or not.

Some years later I think I had simplified my beliefs and when my mother died she too was cremated, a simple casket, hospital gown, Oh God, poor thing arriving in 'heaven', well why not, with the back of the hospital gown waving in the heavenly breezes.

It is amazing the things that drive us at times and finally what choices are made in the name of expediency. Our answers are never quite satisfactory, even for ourselves. Strange, I can cope with my naked soul. I just hope my body is clothed, even in death.

We had not eaten, and I was not in the mood to cook. Too much had crossed my mind. This was Key West, one doesn't think about all the exigencies of life in Key West. I decided to go to the Cuban restaurant nearby on Duval Street. The food is cheap and plentiful, and Cuban. I could sit outside on the terrace and enjoy the evening. I could drink a bottle of wine too. I intended to do just that. My feline mistress seemed content to stay home. She was now curled up on my bed, keeping an eye on me as I dressed to go out.

The food at the Cuban restaurant is simple and good. The wine list is moderate, nothing to celebrate. Although there were couples celebrating; everyone looking young, tanned and relaxed, and with flickering candles in the breeze, terribly romantic. I felt out of place sitting there 'voyeuring' my way through the evening, drinking my cheap wine, eating my food.

The wine relaxed me, and the food sated my immediate hunger. I don't get drunk easily, and I didn't then. However, the wine set my mind, momentarily, free from everything. I ruminated on my extraordinary mind journeys of late and began to realize I had perhaps gone a little mad. Yet in that madness lay a kernel of a bigger 'they.' To call it more would admit it held me in thrall.

We are all trestle bridges of a sort. But you see, we are not. All the other trestle bridges I know about are connected to the next span or to land. It is this particular one that is the metaphor; not connected. The human parallel; 'man is THIS disconnected trestle bridge', each of us alone in eternity, but here, or wherever we are in the fix of things; we are alone. What happens in existence if we have been in love beyond the end of the trestle bridge? Can any part of the passion that drove us be ours to take on the journey through existence?

It is all very well to imagine arriving in our burial finery or our battle gear or naked, but the gem is to find our eternity, and that seems to be unclothed. All of us, from child born moments before death to the eldest living to an ancient age bring with that soul the moments of life in this realm. That babe, as the eldest has been part of existence for all time and this is merely a stopping off place to the next adventure. What it is for us to realize is; how do we fare here? That is what grows the depth of being to carry forth the spark we are to the next realm of the universe.

So far as love beyond realization; it happens rarely and those affected by it must take its power with them, perhaps never to lose its power in existence. It mellows the soul to the extent when next it drops anchor it will have an extra tidbit to inhabit the being it will become. Why, through eternity, do our souls ebb and flow, finding anchors in space? Could it be to grace existence with love, finally? The greater, being, that love and life are one no matter where we are or what form we take.

I must have sat there an inordinately long time because the next thing I realized was the tables were being cleaned and the restaurant help was being restive to 'get on'. I roused myself and apologized for sitting too long. They were very kind, allowing as how it was a beautiful night and I was enjoying myself, etc., etc. I hadn't remembered paying the check, but I had, I also had a 'catty box' to take with me. Madame would be pleased, I thought, she being the cosmopolitan type would probably like the fare.

She did, she ate everything; even the rice and beans. None of this canned tuna for her. Maybe I should have given her a tot of wine to wash down her exotic dinner. No, she seemed content with what she had. Of course, she did the ritual washing.

As I watched her, I wondered, if this is a form of life here. What was this cat in another form? This was getting too far adrift, next it will be cockroaches and other pests that have souls, well, why not, my life was going further from ridiculous to sublime, in a most uneasy manner: everything was up for grabs. I had too much wine, I was imagining too much, and I was being sloppy, personally, mentally and every way I abhor in others. I went to bed!

The next thing I knew it was day, what time? The cat was gone, undoubtedly taking a 'personal day'. I have always hated that term; personal day. It smacks of an employer giving an employee a 'carte', to choose a day to be free of work without responsibility to the paycheck or the job being done. On the other hand, there are times when people 'need' time to handle affairs that arise. Couldn't that be taken without a countdown? As you are hired you are told, "You have five personal days." If you don't use them you have to lump them together, if you can, at the end of December, or lose them: there goes the Christmas party!

I had a hangover. Cheap (or expensive) wine by the bottle ingested augers hangover. I toddled over to the kitchen, which seemed to be a thousand feet in the distance, but in reality was about forty feet as the crow flies, and made coffee. The smell of uncooked coffee gave me assurance I was not dead. Then I went on safari to the bathroom, back through a jungle of furniture, which was ready to nip toes lest you get too close to a snarling upholstered leg as you pass,

then it will pounce on your pinky toe sending paroxysms of pain through your foot leaving you a howling, hopping mess. It didn't happen, thank God! I maneuvered the shoals without incident.

Looking in the mirror was a different matter. Well, I didn't look that bad, but I did look awful. What in God's name had I eaten and drunk? Not that much really, a bottle of wine? Many times, but not like this! So far as the food was concerned; it was peasant food, greasy, which should have helped line my stomach to prevent the alcohol from becoming too much a burden. What was I thinking? I was compensating for something that had no reality beyond over indulgence. So far as the rest of it goes, my brain was scrambled before I had a drop, or a bite to eat. It wasn't the fault of comestibles.

In my miasma, I thought I needed a sail, after coffee, and perhaps some toast. The day was with me, blue with scuddering clouds, good breeze. It was blowing south to north; it would be a straight sail to the bridge, and a tack back down. Such is life.

Madame showed up looking pleased with herself. Hussy! She and I both settled ourselves by the pool. I collected, what I hope, were my thoughts, and labored to work out any meaning in my dreams, which were vivid, to say the least, unto the point of reality where dream and awake come to a point where they are all one.

The sun was heating up and the garden was stirring, mostly with little lizards changing colors to suit on what they perched. The pool was chugging away moving the leaves and twigs fallen in during the night.

I moved to get the skimmer to get them out, but as I moved, I found I was not steady as I thought. It behooved me to sit back and let the moment pass.

Madame looked up at me inquisitively as if to ask if she could be of help. Of course, she couldn't, but it was nice of her to ask. When I seemed settled in my chair with my head on the pillow at the top of the chair, she resumed her duties and ablutions as fits a fastidious being. Actually, she was nearly driving me to do the same, no, not then, not showering and shaving, maybe brushing my teeth. Being in shorts that double as trunks, I decided a swim might do it.

I plunged into the water. It was cool enough to be a pleasure. The cat alarmed at such antics, dove off her chair to prevent being splashed and made for higher ground, to a table far enough away from the pool's edge. It was also shady. She watched me swim laps, somewhat approving, I thought.

I got all the poisons off my skin and felt nearly human. Showers were just great, but a pool really got to the whole thing, only problem was, you had to shower anyway to get the chemicals off.

Now I felt as though I could face the day, and as I checked the clock, which could or not be right, it said 8:30. I must have gotten up about 6:30. Nothing was haunting me at that moment. Trestle bridges were not part of the scheme of things. Maybe a day of layabout for me, eating lightly, drinking nothing but water, coffee or Coca Cola, at least until sundown. It was planned then; quiet and reserved with Miss Puss as company.

The damn phone rang! Now what! Grumpily I answered it having hoped 'it' would go away and hang up but no, insistence was brooding about making a fuss to attend. "Hello!" I said flatly, the voice on the other end sounded not a little plaintive. I was being scolded for not calling. More than that, for not coming north. Had I no sense of obligation? I thought "to what?" I began to feel umbrage being treated like a juvenile delinquent. Good God. I am nearly an old man, and someone dared take me to task for infringement on his or her life? I did not explode simply because it would have upset me. I sure felt like it. As the upbraiding continued, being reminded as I was, that I was inconsiderate among other sins of being hung over and human.

Finally to shut up the noise, and apologize for having missed at least half a dozen events of extraordinary importance, where without my presence simply did not happen, I agreed to return sooner rather than later, but not before I finished up what I was doing, whatever it was.

We hung up but not without a promise extracted, I would turn up at Kennedy Airport in three days; reservations would be made!

I was trapped!

My time to ruminate was effectively done. In my life, I'd never minded too much being herded to what ever social event was being paraded by me. It was part of that thing called 'relationship'. One party of the first part assumed the duty of social arbiter for the second part. Of course, one could go grumpy and renege on the first part's acceptances, but not too often or it would be thought antisocial even if it were to some extent.

Anyway, it was done. I had precious few hours my own to do with. I knew I had to become un-hungover quickly. Voila! I thought just that and I was. I felt fit, the power of positive thinking bailed me out, so, it works on hangovers too! Precious hours, really precious days, but the urgency to mete them out wisely dropped them to hours. Well, time does pass, seconds, minutes, hours, days, weeks, months, years, until you are in all of them, who you are, fleeting, fleeing from time as it passes you into oblivion.

Here I am wrestling with a man in a trestle bridge, a man who comes to me in dreams and lures me to consider larger realms than my life and they want me to be in a place I don't want to be in 72 hours, less now.

I don't want, ever again, to go to New York. There is no earthly reason to go, particularly for one detached as I am from it. I am not satisfied with any aspect of my life. I am not willing to continue the charade being who I am in the eyes of others. There are some who will pass the opportunity to take the presentation of their lives to them to live as they would. (And would, instead opt for the safest harbor and haven surrounding themselves only with all they know and nothing more.) They are the ones who would deny their lives and pay the price the rest of their lives.

I seemed to find strength in resolving to not be one of them any longer. I do not want to go back; there is nothing for me there.

"Then don't go!" The voice was strong, and made me turn to see who was speaking. "What did you say?" "I said, Then don't go, if that is what you mean, don't go!" "Alright, it is easy to say just that, but to do just that is not so easy is it? You come to me in dreams. I chase up to see if you are reality, knowing you are not. Why am I being dogged this way?"

"Because you have asked for enormous change in your life." "I have? When have I done that?" "When you first imagined someone in the bridge. When you first thought of being part of the structure." "There is a man there, living there?" "If you wish." "And who is that?" "Why you, of course, why would there be anyone else?" "Am I the only one living there?" "No, anyone who wants will see himself there, but they are far too few, and then only for a fleeting moment, because to acknowledge the prospect of finding yourself in a trestle bridge is more than most can stand, and they take it as a mirage, but become haunted as if they have missed themselves."

He was gone as usual. After awhile you get used to these things. Piqued with curiosity now, I decided to sail once again to the bridge and see; perhaps for a last time what haunted me. The wind was kind and made me work very little. Of course, the day sparkled, just for me, I thought. Even the cat came along for the ride. If my time were to be limited to others 'frame', I would revel in what I had.

I rounded the Key and there was the frame in the distance, unattached at either end, itself a declining relic of majesty. As I drew near it seemed almost pathetic and strange. I felt sad about that.

What my fantasy had envisioned all along was in reality a decaying bit of steel. I looked for the 'man', he was not there, perhaps had never been. I had to leave room for doubt, that maybe.

I got quite near to the structure, and I peered closely through it. Regardless of its age and decay, it shimmered. I knew there could be a man there, however fleeting, I could see him.   It was not form. It was there. I was not mad at all, and knew I would be willing to go into the unknown with equanimity knowing it is there and accepting of who I am in existence, permitting me to exist as I am in my own eyes without the garment of others making, making me who they expect me to be.

I turned the boat around and set sail. I set sail into the fog of existence where everything is clear on the other side.   There was no fog, it was clear, I held the cat, I laughed and cried and knew I would never be the same again.

THE WAY TO A MAN'S HEART

Ordinarily I don't stop at 'road side' eateries. One never knows what kind of food waits within. I suppose I am one of millions of people who choose familiarity over adventure when it comes to road fare. I have gotten terribly bored with the run of mill fast food, yes, dumps so many of us frequent. There is a certain element of predictable safety in their choice.

I was driving down Route One toward Key West, feeling thirsty and hungry. I was going nowhere in particular, had no room reservation waiting, no agenda, just a get away to some place where I not had been. I was recently made a widower after a long marriage. The pulse of married life stopped. There were so many willing to make life easier that I felt suffocated by the attention.

I packed my bags, actually a bag and golf clubs, and took off. There were cries of dissuasion protesting my leaving friends, children, and grand children. I felt I needed 'my space', so off I went, in a cloud of dust and a hearty Hi Ho Honda! That dates me? That's OK, I'm getting there. I chose the Keys because I had never been there. My wife never wanted to go to Florida. Much less the Keys, it was all too raw; her vision of Florida was Disney Land, and her sense of the Keys was run down bars with drying out alcoholics lying about.

Florida didn't whet my appetite particularly, but I reasoned well enough it wasn't all 'gin', polyester and Mickey Mouse either. I wanted to visit the Keys because they fascinated me with their lore. People I knew who went to the Keys loved them because they seemed to offer space for self absorption, a way of unhurried life, casual enterprise in living, adventure to ferret out and have.

It was probably in this sense that I pulled into the parking lot of the 'Roger's Diner'. It was white, square, nondescript. Definitely a place my wife wouldn't be caught dead in, sorry, you know what I mean. There were some cars in the parking lot, and I reasoned if there were cars, it couldn't be all that bad. I entered the restaurant. It was small. There was counter seating eight and two tables seating four each. It had an open kitchen so you could see the business of food preparation in front of you. It took the place of conversation.

Actually, there was conversation between everyone, the waiter, the cook, the customers, even the dishwasher chimed in though his back was to the customers. I looked at the menu; it seemed to include all the usual things an eatery like this should have, eggs every way, hamburgers every way, sandwiches of the usual sort.

I saw a plate come out of the kitchen that looked very good. I asked what it was and the waiter told me it was braised lamb shank. Braised Lamb Shank? In a road side diner? What else was there, I wondered. The waiter was busy so it gave me time to look around where I was. It certainly wasn't unusual, or was it. Each place was set with cloth. Napkins and cloth place mats. The table ware was heavy stainless steel, and the dishes and glassware not generic Diner Ware. I looked at the back bar and saw cakes and pies that didn't look as though they came from your local bakery. Home made, sure, from a mix? I watched the other customers eating with apparent pleasure. Hey, I knew I hadn't made a mistake!

The waiter brought me a glass of water with ice. I really noticed him for the first time. There was nothing extraordinary about him, except he smiled and asked if I would like to hear the fare of the day. I listened and appreciated what I heard. It was an eclectic menu. I ordered beef stew and remember it was very good. I had desert, I remember well; it was chocolate cake. It absolutely tasted 'home made'. The whole meal was wonderful. I wished my wife could have cooked like that, or would have.

The diners were leaving, it was late for lunch. I ate my cake slowly and engaged the waiter in a bit of conversation. I found out there was no dinner served, just breakfast and lunch. I asked if there were a motel nearby, there was, I decided to look into a place to stay. I wanted to eat here again. I watched the diner prepare to close. Being able to see into the kitchen, I watched them clean up, put away, and make everything 'ship shape'. The waiter came and took my empty place and cup, and would have take the water except I grabbed it to finish it. He asked me if I wanted more, and after rich chocolate cake, I said yes. He filled the glass, again with ice and water. It was something I appreciated, not too many waiters are sensitive to those things. I asked what time the place opened and was told six-thirty in the morning. I said "good night" though it was barely three. The waiter said goodnight too, I thanked him and told him how good the food was. He told me that Roge cooked it all himself, from scratch. "Even the cakes and pies", I queried? "Yes" was the reply. I said "I'd be back", and he said "see ya, then."

I left and looked for the motel and found it. Not bad, certainly not a deluxe resort place, but it had a pool and was near the beach. I could stay awhile and enjoy it. I unpacked, and then went exploring, driving south toward Key West. I began to see what people meant by 'remote' with a sense of peace.

I am sure the Keys are no different from any other community or groups of communities that have day to day problems and people of all stripes living there. It seemed at this moment all the weight of the recent past was removed just looking at the scenery.

I walked on Duval Street in Key West and browsed the tourist shops. There were a couple of art galleries, a few home furnishing shops showed furniture that reflected where you were, light slightly gaudy, colorful, resort feeling. I thought for a moment. A feeling took hold that it might be fun to get a 'little house' and have fun doing it up, just as a place to escape to when I felt pressured to get away. Of course, this was a small fantasy. I wouldn't have the imagination. It had always been done for me. That I liked all of it is moot.

Key West abounds restaurants of all kinds. It abounds Guest Houses, of course it abounds bars and has a glitzy carnival atmosphere. It is after all a tourist Mecca. However not all the people who live there are tourists, and the touristy places are on the main street and down at the piers where cruise liners dock for a few hours to let their passengers look at the 'Key West' of fame. Off on the side streets lies the charm and lore of the Keys. It is there you begin to the feel magic of place. I tell you this in retrospect; it was not my first impression.

I had dinner at one of the restaurants on Duval, and drove back to the motel where I had a good night's sleep, the first in a long time. I was beginning to relax and put the past months behind me.

I woke the next morning looking forward to breakfast. My mind smelled coffee. I showered shaved and put on some shorts, making a mental note that I hadn't brought along enough shorts and casual shirts and to buy them. I didn't put my watch on. It was my first shedding of a 'timed' life. Time was not at that moment important. I did not know what time it was. I was up and rested for the first time in along time. The day was bright and I drove the mile or so to 'Roger's Diner'.

The coffee my mind smelled was the coffee they were serving. The orange juice was squeezed before me, after all this is Florida. The cook waited on me, the waiter had not yet arrived. I was the first customer. I said; "You are 'the' Roger?" He looked at me and laughed; "Yes I suppose I am." "How long have you been here" I asked, "Oh about six months, give or take." "Only six months?" "It seems that way." "How did you get into this?" "By accident, I came in for a hamburger on my way to nowhere. I'd walked out on bad situations. The woman who owns the place and I got to talking. She told me she wanted to go away for a while, she was tired, well, one thing led to another, and I found myself with a years lease on a res- taurant. That's the short version."

"And you, down for a vacation?" "Well yes and no. Like you I'm off to nowhere just moseying along." "Watch out or you'll be in the restaurant business." "Not likely, can't cook worth a damn." "There is something to be said for that, apparently I can. Are you off to any place special or just seeing how the land lays?" "That's one way to put it, I guess. I plan to play a little golf, look at the sights, and take it easy. My wife died about six months ago. Everybody from then on, friends, family were stifling me. I couldn't think clearly, just had to get away." "How come you came down here?" "Don't know, heard about the Keys, it's not a place my wife would ever want to come to, we'd done Europe, and Hawaii, why not the Keys?" "I don't know, why not, it is a place where you can lose yourself that's for sure, look at me, I'm lost as Hell. By the way I don't want to rush you, but are you having breakfast?" We laughed and I did.

Over the next couple of weeks I came in almost every day, and our banter was light and easy. I'd found a couple of golfing buddies, retired Navy officers. When they found out I was alone, I was invited to dinner. It was all very nice; dinner, Bridge, widows. Except that is what I was 'running away' from. Pretty soon it was "Bill, join us for............" I felt terrible about having to accept invitations on the one hand and dishonest pleading a previous engagement. But it came to that. Playing golf with the 'guys' was OK and once in a while having dinner was OK, but the match making was a real drag. I was not ready to even think of that kind of thing.

Occasionally Roger and I would go on his rounds after he closed the 'place'. I really enjoyed that. He was the kind of person who was so relaxed about what he was doing. He would say to me "What's your favorite meal in the entire world?" "I told him that one of them was corned beef and cabbage." He looked at me and said "Corned beef and cabbage?" "That's right" he laughed and laughed, "you got it." Another time he asked what dessert did I crave and I told him, "Apple pie. Now I mean real apple pie, made with apples, no cinnamon or nutmeg, just the taste of apple and butter, I love it!" "Hey, you got it, babe, I'll make it tonight. We can have it for dinner if you like." "You mean you are going to open up?" "No, I can cook in the restaurant without opening up. Come on, what else shall we have? Of course if you are free" Boy was I free!

We had dinner at one of the tables, I brought wine, it was by candle light, very perhaps romantic under other circumstances, but nice and warm. We were just a couple of misplaced men having dinner. The apple pie was the best. Roger turned to me at a point and said; "you know, of course, I'm gay." I told him the thought had crossed my mind and it didn't matter. I used that old saw "some of my best friends are." Truth to tell I did not know gay people in my life. I am sure I have been in their company, have had dealings with them, but no, we did not have gay friends in our life. I never thought about it. And as we sat there having a candle lit dinner it didn't matter. I was some how at peace, and I was happy. We washed up; the rest of the pie was put away for tomorrow's customer. I wished I could have taken it back to the motel, not to eat, just to have.

Roger closed the 'place' Friday night for the weekend. He went to Key West to see the sunset from the top of the Holiday Inn. It wasn't a fixed ritual, but you could be pretty sure he would do that. I asked him why? "Maybe a knight in armor riding a white steed will come charging out here and swoop me up in his arms whisk me away forever to be happy." "Have you anyone in mind." "Oh just a young man I love more than earth." "Is he the reason you've run away?" "One of the reasons, why?" "Oh just wondered."

He was very private about his 'reasons', and I didn't pry. I told him about my life. How I married young, worked at a job, had a family, bought a house, put the children through school, got promoted, made some money, played golf, took my wife on trips. The more I talked the more I realized my life was one of the quintessential lives people all over the world live. I suddenly found myself realizing I'd never had an adventure, right now was the closest I'd ever come out of the rut. I cannot say I was ever 'unhappy' I also can't say I was ever 'happy'. I was gray, well that was the choice I made then. Now was a different matter. I had no one to answer to or for, except as I chose.

I played more golf, went to more dinner parties, danced, played bridge, pool, charades, the whole gambit. The more I did that the more I felt these people were unreal. They thought they were having the adventure of retiring. Oh stop carping, they were to their lights enjoying the golden years. I am sure some of those retirees had had enough adventure to last a lifetime. Most were WWII veterans so they undoubtedly saw a lot of action. Their waiting wives had their adventures too, moving from base to base, from country to country. They were happy to settle by the sea and remember.

On one of our forays into the world of small restaurant shopping, we stopped for a drink at one of the hotels in lower old town. It was very tourist, but it had a pleasant poolside bar. In the course of conversation, Roger began to tell me how he left 'home'. He had been with a man for thirty-nine years, in a relationship that was never easy, except he loved Roger.

The man seemed to have a chip on his shoulder ninety percent of the time. He was, underneath all the unpleasantness, a very generous person. His generosity was negated by his attitudes. He treated Roger well, but Roger was his chatelaine so to speak. Roger is a writer. He read me some of his poetry, which is good. He writes Plays. He is a creative person in other ways than cooking. He spent many years as a volunteer, once even ran for 'office'. So far as being a bread winner he was largely a non contributor. He gave himself to running the household and raising two Children from his lover's marriage. These things didn't seem to matter at the time. He isn't interested in 'things', furniture, property, gewgaws, bric a brac, that kind of thing except for their being part of the household at the moment. In a partnership like that one person ends up with all the assets. His idea of owning property was perhaps a small house in the Keys, away from everybody.

I began to have a sense that this was one for whom possessions were like a noose, the more you had the more the rope tightened until you were strangled by 'things'. What are things anyway, but final give aways to heirs or yard sales. Why are attics full of stuff, except for the appeasement we should not get rid of those things containing memories no one would appreciate but us? You can have memories without all the trappings of mementos. Yet, there are 'things' to be reckoned with. In addition, we reckon with 'things'.

In the Keys, you begin to feel, as you look at the sky, you are on a journey. It has notion of suspension, between the sky and the universe and you are in the middle hung there waiting for the next move in your life. I had been in the Keys for nearly six weeks and began to feel its rhythm. I had no reason to go back 'home'. As a matter of fact home was becoming a remote place more thorn than pleasure to think about. I loved the people, family, friends all the trappings of my 'former' life and I didn't want to lose that connection of my life. I worried about 'things'. I tried to figure how

I could chuck the whole thing easily. There was no answer. Sell the house? Get rid of everything? Give it all away? Put distance between people and me who had been my life? I don't need that house, or that furniture. Lord God, what do people do when they get on with it? What is sacred and what is profane? How will I ever know? What are memories but warped moments we decide are; whether or not they were in fact.

Roger and I developed quite a friendship, never crossing the line of our lives, respecting each other's privacy and intimate thoughts. We discussed everything from, oh, I don't know what to where.

One night we were sitting in his place after coffee, and he told me about his love. He was a young man he'd met one afternoon in the park outside the apartment building he lived in. It was an immediate connection between them, as he said; "I asked him if he were cold, and he lifted his long scarf up in the air and said; "I'm freezing." It was cold, the end of January. When he lifted his arms, it was as if a huge angel spread his wings. It was as if he'd just flown from heaven. He has the bluest eyes you ever seen.

"Our relationship began very tentatively; he never let me know where he lived or even his phone number." I said; "Then he was in the closet? Isn't that what they say about someone who won't admit they're gay?" "Yes, that's the term. Rather than allow himself to be who he is, he fought himself. Rather than accepting himself he wants to become mainstream, and lead a life that will make him respectable, and in doing that would destroy his humanity, himself, and all those he would unwittingly take along with him through life."

"Aren't you being subjective? Don't you want him to come to you and be with you? Some people make a transition, and perhaps lead good lives you can't damn a person for his belief in himself." "Of course not, but I've been through a lot with him, and I know how his mind works, if he tried to lead a straight life, he would die. He is a dreamer, a too free spirit to be shackled. He dreams of adventure, one was to have a place like this. When I met him he didn't know about food, I taught him much." "I am sure you did, you have taught me a lot just being with you, but you see, you are a teacher, a giver to people, that's what makes them love you. You give to everyone." We went on talking. I got quite a picture of both men. The young man, at times capricious, cruel, because he didn't know what to do next. His sudden bursts of rage at everything that touched a spark. Accusations of infidelity, totally unfound, insecurity was such he wouldn't believe Roger; his lies were as great as his imagination would allow. The other one continually put Roger down in order to bolster his ego which had been shattered many years ago by his life and his family. He too raged, lashed out at people, had to control every situation, made himself disliked, Roger for all his culinary magic couldn't get people to spend an evening at dinner. People would demur at an invitation. He would never see what he had done. You could face him with it and he would deny it.

They were alike in many ways. Each was a control 'freak', had to be in charge for fear someone would take control from them. So Roger ran away, as the young man said; "Look at me, I'm runnin' away, I Got my stick, I'm runnin' away. I'm gonna find me another lilly pad." What he didn't know, or wouldn't acknowledge was that he wanted to jump on Roger's lily pad. He said things like; "You're a clingon, you cling on every one. You haven't any money, you're broke." Maybe so, Roger told me he had a minuscule income, not enough to live easily on. He had certainly been dependent on his lover many years, and their life style. He felt put down by that. He felt he'd never made a contribution to any one's life. It was all about money, as usual, it wasn't about the gift of love or life. It made me think how much money kills a relationship. Of course we need to survive, but at what cost. Then there was the morning the young man was driving Roger to the train station and he stopped a cemetery near the station and literally kicked him out of the car saying "Go visit your friends, you'll be there soon enough!" I asked Roger why he put up with that; "Because, he is so afraid of losing me. His safety net was that he would leave me first, he would not let death, or infidelity beat him."

Roger is very much in love with this man. Moreover, he loves his lover of many years too, what a quandary. I asked him how he managed to escape. "I got a small settlement from an accident. I didn't tell anyone about it. I bought my little car, packed my bag, took my papers, bought a notebook computer, wrote them both a note, and took off. I had to prove myself, be self sufficient, able to provide myself an income. I hadn't done it writing. I am too old to do much in the real world; certainly, my resume would be riddled with moth holes. I had done some pretty interesting things with my life, I wasn't always a housewife. That is another hundred stories. It has not been a dull life." I didn't think it was that dull. Perhaps not unusual. I seem to remember some of the same predicaments, even in my own life but that too is another story.

We sat there for a while. It was getting late. I knew Roger had to be up at the crack of dawn. We stood up and faced each other. I looked at him. He was an old man. Of course he was. I am a bit younger than he is, not much. I wondered what he had to attract two men into his life. I realized as I looked at him it was love, giving, acceptance of the person, a smile, laughing eyes. Then I knew he attracted a lot of people, store keepers, strangers who asked directions, second helpings, kindness. One of the big lily pads. I left, he hugged me goodnight, I felt wonderful.

The next day we were driving to Key West and I turned to him and said; "Roger, I think I am falling in love with you." He laughed "That's sweet of you Bill, it's your lunch." "No, I don't think so, Roger. Last night while we were talking, it came over me. I think I want to spend the rest of my life with you." "You've got to be kidding. After all the things I told you, you want to spend the rest of your life with me?" "I think so." "I don't have any money. This thing with the restaurant will probably be over in six months. After that I don't know what I want to do, or even where I want to go. Do you want to live like a vagabond?" "Sure, why not, I don't have a lot of money either. I have a house I can sell. I have a pension, Social Security, a bit of a nest egg. We can make it no matter where we go."
"What about your family your friends your life back there, what about that?" "I don't owe any one any more of my time or money.

My children are doing well; my friends will be there if I want to see them occasionally, I am free to do with my life as I please." "And me? After telling you all about me, do you think I am free? I mean emotionally. I have a lot of baggage. I love that young man. I want that old man to be my best friend. That is where we are finally, I am not free. I am flattered, but not emotionally free."

"I know you'd like to have that young man ride down the street in shining armor and swoop you up into your dreams. It might happen. I also know you would love for that other man to become wonderful and loved by all. That too could happen. The reality is; you are here and neither one of them are, but I am. I don't know how this all came about. I have never considered myself 'gay' for a moment. I have never lusted after or looked at men other than the way men look at each other as people or friends. My love for other men has been in that realm of friend, comrade, confrere, buddy, bonded male, whatever. A great part of my life ended about the time a great part of yours ended. We became faced with changing lives. Life is not meant to be static. An awful lot of people, like me, have lived their entire lives without ever having an adventure. When I came into your diner that day, I was at loose ends. I only knew that when I had my meal I wanted to return. I noticed as I came in regularly, there were other men who came in just as regularly. I watched those guys. In their way, they are in love with you too. You give them something they don't get elsewhere, its love, you tell them you love them the way you feed them and care how the food is fixed. I don't know what it is, but, if the other two idiots don't see it, you give to everyone, that they have to continually put you down and beat your senses and hurt you, that is because they are afraid to let themselves go with you. You are an adventurer, a dreamer for whom life is a stepping stone, yes, Roge, I love you, as you think about that, don't throw this baby out with the bath water. If the young man does sweep you off your feet, I will lose the possibility of some sort of future with a person I fell in love with over a piece of chocolate cake, but I will know what chocolate cake is supposed to taste like."

"Bill, what can I say, it's so far out in left field. You don't know the first thing about 'gay' love; you've never had sex with a man."

"Roger, it does not take a rocket scientist to put two together. What I can't figure out, I feel sure you'll help me with, in every way. Look, I'm nobody's beauty, but I'm no slouch either. We can work this out, day by day. You wouldn't be landing on my lily pad. I'm landing on yours. Let's face it, I'm not in love with men, I'm in love with you. You happen to be a man, so what, at my age I'm game for love no matter how it happens."

"Bill, suppose that young man does come swooping down on a white charger, or that old curmudgeon becomes sweetness and light, what then" "Well, I guess I'll have to play it as it lays God willing, a hole in one."

THE MAN WHO SAT
IN A CHAIR
BY THE SEA

He was an old man. How old you would not guess because he seemed ageless, and was. He lived by the sea in a warm place where breezes caress the land. His, was not much of a house, a shack really, weather worn with the time it had been standing. It had seen hurricanes, storms and rough seas wash all around, and it stood through all.   Were you to look inside you would see a very plain home, bare floors, a table or two, some chairs, and a bed.   Gauze curtains fluttered at the windows more to keep mosquitoes out than to ensure privacy. He lived a simple life. He lived by light of day. At night he retired, or looked to the sky for omens of the future.

When he needed 'things' he drove his old car to the village nearby. People went out of their way not to become personal or ask questions. The old man ventured out of necessity. He had few needs, but those he had he would get. When he met people in the little village by the sea, he was smiling and friendly. He would chat for a bit then get in his old car and drive off. They surmised and wondered. Who is the man who lives at the end of a road on a spit of land leading nowhere but into the sea? Where did he come from? There were no answers. No one knew the truth, what ever it was. It was not terribly important to them. Most of the people in the village were a maverick sort anyway. For them to become involved, more than passing, unless there was a need, was not their nature of living.   People who live in remote areas, and by the sea are usually the sort who want their privacy. Socializing was going to the bar drinking beer, talking about things of common interest.

Every now and then, someone would drive out to the spit of land to 'sort of check things out'. The house stood, and all seemed serene around it.   Sometimes they saw the old man sitting on a chair by the sea, just sitting there, and seeming to look into the far reaches of space. They would drive away as if they were off track.

He walked the beach and studied the sea to know what it held for him that day. He sat in the shade of the porch in the mid day, swam in the sea in the afternoon, and waited.

Since there was no one there to see him wait, no one knew he waited. As a tree in the forest makes no sound we can discern when it falls, how would you know what an alone old man would do?

He was a born searcher. In his youth, he had been many things, done many things, and experienced many loves. Searchers are people who spend lives looking for knowledge and meaning. They express themselves in many ways, in many fields of endeavor. Theirs is never a final answer to any question about the universe. As soon as a discovery is made, there are more questions. Answers are themselves questions. Every answer begs definition, and asks the question nearest it. There will never be a definitive answer to existence. It simply is.

As for them who would inquire of existence its meaning, no matter the subject, they will have nothing satisfactory. Discovery is moot. The old man spent many lifetimes looking for answers to the progress of the ephemeral soul of man on earth. The creators of existence, asked him to define man on earth, and why the animal, man, should continue to have the soul of existence over all the other creatures on earth.

The animal man can operate without a soul as he goes through his life. Man speaks, animals communicate, man builds, animals and birds build. There is no significant difference in all creatures, except animal man, was given the soul of creation and existence in the universe. Why is man deserving of a soul above all other creatures? In his tenure on earth, from the beginning of time, man has constantly abused its power.

They asked if man should continue to have the one thing that was eternal as creation. The old man was chosen by the gods of creation to prove man, the animal, deserved the privilege of possessing the essence of creation. The old man knew the key to the answer lay in the moment of love man felt for all things around him. If it could be proved, there was love on earth then, man, the animal, would deserve to possess the soul of existence in the universe and the earth would live. He lived in many places; and saw in his travels, so much disregard for the land and so little regard for humanity and life. He concluded man would certainly destroy the planet, and that would ultimately destroy him, and all other living things. There was no reason for the soul of man in existence to continue on earth in 'man'.

One day the old man met a young man. He hoped the young man had the vision to accept the mystery of what he learned. The old man realized he had to convince the young man all he told him was true. The young man questioned, and rightly, for what he learned pertained to things far beyond what he understood and went beyond his belief.

The young man had to tear down all the old man said. No matter what it was, he had to equate what he believed from the knowledge he knew. If he believed the old was man who he was, it would fly in the face of his understanding. If he accepted who the old man said he was, he could not but question.

The young man never understood; messengers sent to earth are human beings, subject to all things human. Belief is recognition this human being is a messenger. Man has never understood we are more reflection of who we love and being reflection give the loved one a mirror to see himself. The mirror has two faces. He has not learned love is unconditional. It is the axiom of the meaning of love. It is difficult to love without prejudice.

Man is bound by one tenet; love thy neighbor. No one does. No one is tolerant of another. It came to this; there is no universal love on earth at this time or at any other time in history. Men are bound to greed and distrust of others not of their ilk. Bound to greed and hate to where there is starving and inhumane conditions.

The old man sat waiting for the time to tell The Seven Gods of creation the soul of man on earth was as good as dead. He had been waiting many centuries. He had lived a very long time. He had seen it all and remembered. Time is not that thing which propels existence. Time is that thing we in existence wait upon to happen. The old man bathed in the sea and in a small pond that bubbled forth-fresh potable water. It was from the pond he took the water he needed to live. His life was open to the elements, being open, he enjoyed all there was to live.

He recognized the importance of his mission to the gods of creation and existence. To them time was a nonce. To him it was several lifetimes. It was with great sadness he realized he must tell them evil in men's hearts out weighed their good.

To continue the placement of man's soul on earth would be folly in the animal man. He would never learn generosity, kindness, or fellowship with his fellow man.   Better to give man's soul of eternity to whales or porpoises. They have what it takes in love for fellow creatures.   Their aim is not to destroy, but to enhance life and preserve the planet. This cannot be said of the animal man.

The young man long deserted him for the pleasures of his world and for people who accepted him. The old man was a myth. Someone he never met. Now and then, he unconsciously touched a small stone given him, and remembered for a moment. The young man had to believe the old man was a liar. If he was not then all he had been told was too frightening to behold.

The soul of man on earth challenged to other destinies and the earth becoming barren without the soul of life.   Man knows the other planets in his solar system are barren. Does he realize perhaps, they were once homes to animals like him?

You cannot count the stars; therefore, you cannot count the planets in existence.   It is no great thing to send souls to other reaches and to the edge of time. Man is learning there are many more elements that make up existence than could ever be imagined. Yet he destroys his home.

Day after day, the old man waited for the time when he would tell The Gods what should happen to the soul of man on earth. He knew what his answer would be. He knew life on earth would be better without mans' soul. He had given existence on earth nothing.

The time had come to meet with the seven Gods. It was time to tell them. The Gods would decide. What he recommended would make their minds. He was not happy because it was all encompassing. The over whelming fact is; the breadth and depth of humanity is not deserving of their souls on earth. There are few, undoubtedly, who are not like the others. They do not outweigh those who are determined on the destruction of the earth. The tipped side of the scale has no regard for humanity or creation to make life viable.

Hate is too terrible. Easy destruction of life for all creatures is desolation. Why should the Gods grant soul to man who destroys? Let man be committed to another life form and let him learn, another lesson in his recreation. He has not learned anything in this time of his creation.

The old man appeared before the Gods who gathered above the earth.

One day, rising in the East a great wave headed toward land. The time had come. This was more than a wave. From where he sat in the heavens, he saw the souls of man on earth swept up with the force of water. The wave approached. He accepted he was off to life on another plane of existence, as were all the souls swept up in the wave. The wave passed over all things. The shack was swept away.

There was change on earth. All things lived according to their species. However, humanity as we know it was dead. What was left was a primeval place where life would live without the soul of man. One day in a very long future, perhaps those souls flown would return after they had lived many thousands of lives learning love is the only motivation in existence.

At this time and from this time, the animal, 'man', lived without conscience on earth until he was swallowed with his rage of greed and destruction.

It was burned throughout his body and he never lived as 'man' on earth as we know him again.

In the stars are the answers to all life. 'Man' as we know him is dust in the eyes of creation. It is from dust the Gods created man, and it is to dust he returns.

YESTERDAY AND AFTER

Let me tell you a small story pertinent to nothing in history or even to me except it happened and is remembered. Why I will never know. What happened that summer before World War II in Maine is a capsule of a moment and of people who lived then.

We went to visit my Aunt Elsie in York Harbor, which was different in those days as the abacus is to the computer today. York Harbor then was a small village with the general store and two summer hotels catering to summer people from Boston or points south. It was a genteel time just before the war when the most that could happen to ruffle the quietude of a lazy summer day was the arrival of guests from another place.

Well, that year did see the sinking in May of the submarine Squalus (SS-192) which held our undivided attention. Everyone bemoaned the loss of life, but was thankful 33 men survived. The submarine was raised over the summer and over-hauled and went on to serve in WW-2. It was renamed the Sailfish. Her crewmembers dubbed her the 'Squalfish', and it was thought to be unlucky. She did earn distinction by sinking the Aircraft Carrier IJN Chuyo, which was carrying 21 captured members of the Sculpin. One American survived.

I was twelve and it had little impact on my life. My life was about going to the beach, having lunch, and picking blueberries for a pie for dinner. The new Irish cook was not well versed in cooking much less New England fare. My mother taught her some of the rudiments, and gave her a Fanny Farmer cook book to read as a bible. Fanny Farmer was the bible for Irish cooks newly come to Boston for many years. It was also the cooking bible for young New England married's in the early twentieth century. No bride started home making without one. Looking back at the recipes and rereading them even today, they seem the soul of simplicity, in the old book. We had the 1928 version. Although the recipes were not at all adventurous by today's cuisine, they were how we lived then.

After dinner, we retired to the drawing room where we read or played cards. My aunt had a wind-up phonograph that used cactus needles or steel needles to play the records. You had to sharpen the cactus needles with the smooth side of an emery board every couple of plays. They did not wear out the record grooves as readily as the steel needles did, and therefore were thought preferable. Records, in those days were very expensive.

My mother bought the new reading/recording of Brahms Second Piano Concerto played by Serge Rachmaninoff and the Philadelphia Orchestra conducted by Leopold Stokowski. It was a set of 11 or 12 two-sided records. After each side was played the machine had to be rewound, and the next side played for five or six minutes.

Friends in New York owned a Capehart. This was a radio/record-player combination. If it worked as it should, the record changer would turn the record over automatically for the next side to play. The Capehart was electric and did not have to be wound, ever. We heard really funny stories about various Capeharts that were terribly temperamental and played only music they liked. There is a story told of a Dean at either Harvard or Yale who owned a Capehart. He loved Gilbert and Sullivan; the Capehart did not and threw those records across the room much to his disgust.

The Brahms concerto became almost a hymn for me. I am sure I had it-memorized note for note. That music sustained me through all the years of turbulent growing up, and way beyond. In all my dark years, I recalled the first bars of the concerto, and somehow, what ever was my sorrow or stress, the music held me together. Even to this day, when I hear it I am brought back to my first hearing that gentle summer.

A friend brought Aunt Elsie some moonstones from Asia. It was decided we would make the trip to Boston, to Shreve, Crump and Low, to have a necklace designed for the stones to be worn when my aunt wore her grey velvet afternoon robe, the winter one trimmed with Chinchilla at the sleeves. In those days ladies dressed for tea. In winter, the great houses in Boston were often drafty, so everyone dressed warmly. I had three dowager aunts, who in their youth had been presented to the Prince of Wales, later Edward VII. They were known as the "Three Graces", not by everyone. It was an assumed style on their part. As I remember it told me, they were tall and angular, and had long necks, which, as I understand from my Aunt Carolyn, their younger by a lot half-sister, they referred to as swan-like. According to Carolyn, they lay about in tea gowns all day long admiring their visages mightily. True or not, I do not know, Carolyn obviously did not care too much for her sisters. My Aunt Lucy received the Croix de Guerre for her work in Belgium during the First World War running an orphanage for young children. She was a great friend of Queen Marie of Romania. They got around in very high society not only in Boston but in Europe as well.

We headed off to Boston on a fine morning to get the moonstones set. The drive was not difficult, as I remember it; we arrived in Boston, at Shreve's, as they said then. The door attendant took the car and my aunt went into the store. My mother, brother and I would go and pedal a Swan Boat on the Common. We agreed to meet at the Ritz Carlton for lunch. The Boston house was closed for the summer, and there were no servants to fix lunch. My grandfather, who had died a few years before this time, had an apartment at the Ritz. The apartment was kept for several years as a convenience so we could repair there to go to the bathroom, wash our hands, and if necessary, wait for my aunt to arrive. My aunt closed her Charles River Square house and moved into the Ritz when war broke out. My grandfather also had a house on Fairfield Street, which had been closed for many years. It was given to Boston University, and became a dorm.

The day was summery and bright; it being Boston, it was not particularly hot, although Boston gets hot in August. We boated, and walked through the gardens, which were world-famous for their beauty.

At one o'clock, we went across the street to the Ritz. We were ushered into the dining room where my aunt was waiting for us. She seemed particularly pleased with her morning, the necklace was designed, and there were enough stones for a brooch. The whole thing was to be done in sterling which would show the stones off to their best advantage. She would take it to Palm Beach that winter and wear it with a grey silk dress, probably for tea. Then when she went to Majorca to visit my aunt, in the spring, she would take it there too. It sounds like these were her only jewels, not at all; these were just her latest acquisition. She was very pleased with them.

My grandfather had two wives. The first time he married was after the Civil War, he having been born in 1840. He married about 1868, to a woman named Brown; her family was in the investment business. Their company became Brown Brothers Harriman. They had four daughters who styled themselves the "Four Graces". One died and they became the "Three Graces".

When his wife died my grandfather married again, probably in 1895, to my grandmother, who was a King, a New York family, famous historically speaking. Rufus King is well documented, as are his sons and daughter. My grandmother, Sally, was no spring chicken when she married my grandfather, but she bore him four more children, this time three boys and a girl. My father was the youngest, born in 1902. I am told his mother was 54 at the time and my grandfather was 63. People find that hard to believe, but it is true.

My grandmother died when my father was 12, and it became his half sisters' duty to raise him, his brothers and sister. My grandfather had no truck with that sort of thing. He was an inventor, and somewhat successful. He and his brother worked with Edison, and as the story was told, it was a hair from his brother's beard that Edison used first as the filament for his first bulb. My grandfather invented the thermostat for an entirely different purpose than what it became used for ultimately that invention among others.

A small anecdote: My parents were married in 1925 at the insistence of Helen Menken, who was playing in Denver at the time. She became one of my Godmothers a couple of years later. I think she was married to Humphrey Bogart at the time. The only way my mother and father could travel with her troupe on its tour, then back to New York, was with benefit of matrimony. They eloped on Mother's Day much to the consternation of my maternal grandmother and great-grandmother. My mother had been engaged to one of the richer heirs in Denver, wedding planned, the works. It was to be a social event. My great-grandparents were part of the founding society that made Denver. Therefore, it was a blow to all concerned when my parents eloped. Everyone thought they despised each other.

They got home to New York in September and set up housekeeping. My mother was tiny and very beautiful. She had the best education money could buy and her clothes came from Worth in Paris. She spoke French like a native, had dark hair and blue eyes. My father was ordered to Philadelphia to my Aunt Florence's house to have my mother introduced to the family, then to Philadelphia society, perhaps.

They arrived on a cold November day, dreary to say the least. My tiny mother was ushered into the drawing room with my father, who was not the tallest man, and they sat on a deep down filled sofa awaiting the arrival of the Three Graces. Arrive they did, and as my father later put it, 'they stood in front of the fireplace with a fire in it swishing the back end of their gowns to get the warmth up into their bodies, all the time questioning my mother about her pedigree; of course, they were farting up the chimney'. My father always laughed at that story which he told with relish. The sight of these ladies, all well over six feet, fanning the fire with their floor-length velvet robes, farting up the chimney, must have been a sight.

In 1916 my father's two brothers went off to war, my Uncle Jack becoming the youngest Naval Officer; I am not sure whether it was of the war or ever. He weaseled his way into the Navy by lying about his age, which might have been 16. That left Carolyn and my father with my Aunt Elsie, Aunts Florence and Lucy having gone off to do their part.

It is this aunt, Elsie, who we were with at the Ritz. My parents, poor as church mice at this time, were the poor relations up for the summer. The first half was to be spent with my Aunt Elsie and the second half in Kittery with Aunt Lucy and her husband, Dr. E. Petrie Hoyle, a white haired and rather forbidding man whose passion was sweet peas. There were bowls of sweet peas all over the living room. The smell was wonderful. He took a fresh bowl of the sweet peas to my aunt's bedroom every morning they were in bloom. The gardeners kept a fresh supply of other flowers all over the house. But no one upstaged the sweet peas.

The Hoyles had a Steinway concert grand piano, which had a player attachment to it. I discovered Beethoven's Moonlight Sonata played by Vladimir Horowitz among the rolls of music. I took a great fancy to that piece of music. I suppose the first movement held a great romantic illusion for me. As the Brahms Second Piano Concerto haunted my ear and my soul, so did the Moonlight Sonata haunt my newly discovered puberty, romantically, of course. I played it so often I was restricted to once a day, and that to be at a time when there were minimum people in the house, including the servants. This meant afternoons when everyone was off doing something, and the servants had a few hours, before dinner, to themselves.

My aunt kept to her bed in the mornings breakfasting there, going over the mail, and planning every one's day, menus, shopping and the like. As I remember her, she was a bosomy person, unlike my other aunts who were bony and slim. She had grown heavier in the ensuing years and was nice to hug.

One morning in an effusive rush, I knocked on her bedroom door. I had a great idea. She bade me enter, and she was indeed in bed wearing silken bed jacket with a piece of gauze net wound around her head like a turban. That was to keep her hair in place while she slept. I never quite understood that; her maid 'did' her hair every morning in a chignon.

Anyway, bade as I was, I went to her bed and snuggled up to her. She let me climb beside her and she put her silky arm around me and asked what was the flurry to see her before she descended for the day. "Aunt Lucy", I said, "please don't take this wrong, because I don't want you to die, not ever, but if you should, may I have the

Steinway, and the dining room chairs?" Her dining room chairs were magnificent, hand made in Spain some hundred years before. She laughed and said to me in a merry voice, "My dear, thank you for not wishing me to die too soon, but don't you think there are others, your cousins for instance, who would like the piano much as you? Why, you do not know how to play the piano. You just like it because it has rolls of music and someone else plays the music for you. If you knew how to play, then I would consider giving you the piano, if you would learn to play well. So far as the chairs are concerned, they go with the table, and you'd have to have a very large dining room for all that, however we shall see."

However, I am ahead of the story. We were in Boston at the Ritz Hotel for lunch. My Aunt Elsie, an angular aunt, was effusing about her moonstones and how well they would look on several costumes, now that she thought about it. A waiter hovered waiting for the order. She waived him aside telling him she would let him know when we would order.

She told us she planned to visit Lucy and Peter in Majorca that winter, and go on to Paris to visit various friends, this was 1939, and the war had not begun.

I remember waiting to see the King and Queen of England on their visit to the United States, in May or June and standing for hours on the Westside Highway at 23rd Street waiting for just a glimpse of royalty. Believe it or not, everyone was dressed in their best for the occasion. I remember a Scotsman in his kilt with all the accessories, waiting with us.

They did drive by, finally, with a motorcade of New York's finest citizens. Governor Lehmann, and Mayor LaGuardia, I believe rode with them. The visit to Hyde Park was to come later in the day. I would love to say it was a royal progress. It wasn't. They sped by, it seemed, probably 30 miles an hour. The Queen held her hat and waved at us, it was an open car. It was over, just like that. The Scottish gentleman, kilt and all, was happy though.

I'd rather hoped the motorcade would have stopped, the Queen having seen me, and asking the driver to stop the car, would get out and shake my hand. Not at all. They sped on.

My aunt would visit her titled friends in the winter of 1940. As it turned out, she didn't. She knit furiously for her friends in England, and sent packages abroad with the State Department. I don't think she ever went to Europe again, I'm not sure, but I think she died during the War. In any case this was to be the last summer I would ever see my aunt. I was shipped off to school.

One of the things I determined was to learn to play the piano. With the "maybe" of the Steinway, and perhaps the chairs in my future, I felt there was some merit to earning them, perhaps not the chairs. My aunt and uncle had so many possessions to leave various cousins and his only child, by a previous marriage. Petrie Hoyle had been a doctor in the British Army in India, and as such carried a demeanor of reticence entirely earned by his standing in society.

One night there had been a dinner party. It was a distinguished company. After dinner, the guests and their hosts repaired to the verandah for coffee and brandy. Everyone was dressed in summery eveningwear. Ladies in long dresses and gents in summer whites. Of course everyone smoked cigars and cigarettes. It was derigueier. I have not a clue what they talked about, probably money. They always talked about money. They were Republicans. That was among themselves. Money was never mentioned in general company. I do remember one thing; one of the guests had a new Buick, got under unusual circumstances. They had owned a 1938 Buick Roadmaster and had custom seat covers made for it. Apparently, a friend of theirs came along and admired the seat covers so much they agreed on a trade; a 1939 Buick Roadmaster for the 1938 Roadmaster with the seat covers.

I stayed behind. I went to the piano and they heard Beethoven's Moonlight Sonata. When I was done, I was complimented on my playing. My Aunt Lucy said wearily, that was not the young man playing; it was Vladimir Horowitz, on a music roll. I said, "No, it was me who played the piece." I had spent that part of the summer learning the fingering Horowitz used and had obviously played it nearly perfectly. Of course, I had to prove it was me, so I proved it. I played the Sonata for them as my audience. It was the only time in my life I was able to do it. Not only that, but I never played it again.

Not to say the least, I did not, so far as I know, inherit the piano. Nor did I take piano lessons.

Some years later, my brother, then in the Navy, went to visit my aunt and uncle in Majorca. They had moved there permanently after the war. Their house was an 18th century villa. Not large and impressive, I am told. One year there were terrible rains. There were monstrous mudslides, and one day their villa, undermined by the rains, slid down the mountain with them aboard. I presume the piano and chairs went with them. So much for inheriting a family fortune.

The last week in August we were driven to Boston to catch the Eastern Steamship Liner City of New York back to New York. It was the calmest night on the Cape Cod Canal; people lined the banks to catch the breeze, and I got unbearably seasick. I was to go off to school in Lake Placid. My mother's father died leaving her money, which assuaged the fit of impecuniousness we had been living with. We went home to River House again without feeling poor.

Aunt Elsie had decided we should order our lunch. She was in a merry mood, and told us we could have anything we wanted on the menu to eat. My mother ordered, I could not tell you what, probably a club sandwich; the Ritz was famous for its club sandwiches. She probably ordered one for my brother too. Then it was my turn. I had been given a carte blanche! I intended to use it. In those days, the most expensive thing on the luncheon menu was turtle soup. I had never had turtle soup, but it was five dollars a serving, and that was the attraction. I had been given permission to have any thing my heart desired, and I would have turtle soup. I said to the waiter, "I will have turtle, please". My mother looked positively aghast. My brother, seeing horror on my mother's face began to giggle. My look was, I am sure, I have got my way at last.   My aunt looked slightly ruffled, but not undone and said, "Little boys do not eat turtle soup. You will have a club sandwich as your brother is having. You will not have turtle soup!"

THE ISLAND, THE PILLAR
AND THE IVY

Once upon a time, in the middle of the sea, there was a little island. There was nothing at all on this island except a pillar. Many years before the island had been part of other land and the pillar was part of a building. Once many years ago, there was a giant earthquake in a land that sank to the bottom of the sea leaving only the little island with the pillar standing. It may have happened this way, but no matter what may have happened, all there was left was the island and the pillar standing in the middle of the sea.

Since it stood in the middle of the sea, it was constantly battered by wind and weather, and when the sea was angry and rough it sometimes washed right over the island. Some how through all the battering the island existed and the pillar stood.

One day, flying on a high wind, a small seed fell at the base of the pillar. The soil of the island was sandy, and not too good for growing things, but the seed was tired of flying and could not move another inch, beside if it did it might have gotten lost in the sea forever. As it lay there a gentle wind blew and some light rain fell and the seed planted itself in the soil comfortably. The sun shown and some rain fell and in a little bit a small green leaf one day popped its head above the surface of the ground. From the shape of the leaf it was easy to see it was an ivy plant. The weather was kind to it and allowed it get a hold in the sandy soil. Soon it began to throw tendrils and grow root. New leaves formed, and in a short time, compared to time, as the island and the pillar knew it, it began to climb up on the pillar's base as ivy plants are wont to do.

The pillar did not take any particular notice of this little creature who invaded his precious space, simply because he never looked down. The island knew, of course, and was glad to have a bit of green there. It felt it was surely an addition to the island because it would, as it grew prevent soil erosion. And soil was a precious thing. The island remembered when it was part of a larger land mass and was not an island at all.

Before the earthquake, the pillar had been part of a temple dedicated to a long forgotten God. It had a forest surrounding it. But invaders took all the trees away until the land looked barren. It had taken men many years to decimate the forest and that is why there was a temple and a town. During the time, they were there the place where the temple stood was inland from the sea.

Then one day the earth rumbled and there was great movement as the earth became angry at the invaders of the beautiful island and sent them all into a great abyss and opened chasm. The only thing to ever tell there had been a civilization was the little bit of earth and the pillar. All the rest vanished into the sea. Because there was nothing to entice men to that spot, no ship ever sailed near. A ship could see the pillar standing in the distance, and men remembered the tale of the land that sank beneath the sea. It was a legend.

For many years the pillar stood defiant against the elements and sur- vived. It did not know why it wanted to survive, but it did. The island was dependent on the sea and the weather to keep it steady and not wash away what little there was left. The pillar was proud, the island humble. The pillar stood defiant against nature. The is- land hoped for survival.

Now there was this little bit of ivy growing. The island was pleased it had a friend. The pillar took no notice of the event. It had stood there through all the upheaval. It needed nothing to help it stay. Of course it never occurred to the pillar that another earthquake might come along and shake it down to rubble. It was a fact; it was the last remnant of a civilization that once reigned.

The island, of course knew this too, but it felt if providence would look its way, it could grow a little, and perhaps once again become a land mass men would visit. It was dubious however, remembering what happened before. Maybe it would begin to grow larger and larger. Maybe once again it would become a large island where trees would grow. Once again men's greed would decimate the land to where the earth would create a giant earthquake and all would be lost, again. All this was a dream, for any of it to happen would take years, and whereas the island was as eternal as the earth and the seas, no matter where it was, the pillar was subject to the whims of weather.

It was a grand dream for the island, it liked the company of trees and grasses, and flowers, these things brought birds to nest, and the birds brought seeds which when planted would grow and the island would grow. It was a nice thought. His memories were stirred of his past.

Now here was a start, a little ivy plant was running about like a happy child throwing tendrils and leafing. In nice weather, which it was at that time, it doesn't take much for an ivy plant to grow.

One day the pillar took notice of the ivy plant growing up his base. He looked down with disdain and asked, not hospitably, "Who are you?" The island replied pleasantly, "Why, it's a bit of ivy come to visit for a while." The pillar ever aware of its territory exclaimed, "A bit of ivy, indeed, what is it doing here?" "Visiting." replied the island. The ivy wanted to introduce itself to the pillar, but was stopped by the island with a shush, "I'll explain later when he is not paying attention" The pillar replied, "I am always attentive, what else have I to do?" "Well, you didn't notice when the seed fell, and you didn't notice when the ivy began to grow, did you." "I have far more important things to consider than seeds that fly through the air, or take root in your soil, mine is a very important task, and I am ever mindful what it is." The ivy asked, "What is it?" "Well of course, it is to be mindful what I am." The island said; "It doesn't seem to me that only to be mindful is terribly important in the mix of things, considering there is nothing to be mindful of here." "What do you mean there is nothing to be mindful of here? I look in every direction out over the sea, I am mindful of that. I see ships sail by on the horizon. I am mindful of that, there is very much to be mindful of as I stand against the time and tide." The ivy considered this for a moment; "Then to be mindful of all things around is the important thing?" "Well, wouldn't it be, how else can you manage the affairs of state?" The island countered; "what state? That was lost a long time ago in the great happening, when everything was lost, even the land that was beneath us. Not to mention the people and the trees and the ships and the buildings." "Yes, but you see, you and I are still here, and now we have this interloper growing all over us. Someone has to run and manage things, and since I am tallest, it must be me."

"Not at all", said the island, "If anyone should be in charge, it should be me, if for no other reason, without me there would be no you. I am the foundation that keeps you standing."

"Perhaps you are right," conceded the pillar, "you are, after all, the elder to both of us, the ivy and me, but, you see, I am taller, I see more than either one of you, therefore, I should be the king, I see more than you do." The ivy said; "That is all very well, I may be a young sprout compared to either of you, but I am alive, I can live and travel. My seeds can fly as I was flown in the winds, I can be anywhere life will have me." The island said; "Without me neither of you could exist. The sea and I are the foundation of all there is here. It is silly for three dependent equals to even imagine who is wiser, taller, or has the power to rule nothing. The sea has the power to rule. It can obliterate us with a wave, and after that I will still exist. I don't care who is king. Either one of you can be crowned for all it matters to me."

"Not only that" said the ivy, "but without each other we are nothing here. Maybe the pillar could stand a little taller, if earth would 'mmmph' itself a bit higher, I could grow a bit faster and what would be seen from the sea would be an inviting place for birds and seeds to fly to, and in time maybe we could become a haven instead of being barren as we are now."

"That is up to the both of you" said the island, "I would like to grow and perhaps in time become large enough to become home to all creatures. But as we all know, we can be destroyed in a moment as we were before, and all we have worked for naught. No land or society is a match for the boiling earth or maddened sea; they can destroy everything they choose. They are the supreme masters of what and who we are, we are nothing to them."

"Then we must ask the sea for protection" opined the ivy, "The Sea speaks to no one. It is its own force and goes where it pleases and how. True there are currents and flows, ultimately he is his own master." said the island.

The ivy pondered this for a while, and then asked the island if no one ever spoke to the sea. The island said no one has ever spoken to the sea because the sea never stops moving and therefore can't have conversations.

"Then I will speak to the sea. If no one has ever spoken to it how do they know it never speaks?" "Do as you wish." said the island, "but I believe you will hear nothing from the sea except a great swoosh as it travels by."

The ivy called out; "Great Sea will you hear me? I have many questions for you to answer if you would but respond." The great Sea without pausing spoke, "What question could you have of me?" The ivy said a bit tremulously, "Would you answer a question for me?" "Certainly, if I know the answer." "Then why are we subject to your whim?" "You are not subject to my whim at all." "Then why are we so afraid you will destroy us?" "Who is 'us', asked the great sea?" "Why, the island the pillar and me" replied the ivy. "I have no power to destroy anything" said the great sea. "But it is you who sweeps over the land when you are angry. It is you who sinks ships and boats in great storms, and make men vanish under your turmoil. You are the most powerful of all the forces we know." "I am only a force driven by another; I am driven by the moon. She creates the tides. I flow as I do because she wills it. I am but a small sea. She drives the oceans beyond me, and creates havoc in her moods. If you would know more, ask her, and if she answers, you will know more than I know, for I know nothing except that I flow." With that, the sea moved on.

"How can we ask the moon?" asked the ivy. The island replied "Well, you asked the sea and he replied." The pillar, ever standing, looking out to the rim of the world, thought a moment, and said; "If the sea, which is the largest thing we know, tells us he is a small thing, driven by the moon, and there are larger seas beyond him, what is where we are?" "Simply where we are" said the island. "We are nothing in the world we live in." "Then what are we to do?" "There is not too much we can do but be here until all the fates decide otherwise" replied the pillar. "Goodness knows I am fragile enough and given to the whims of the winds and seas, I was once part of something else, and now I am part of nothing but this place." "So are we all" said the Ivy "We are all part of nothing except as we are to each other, without each other we wouldn't exist."

"You spoke to the great sea, do you suppose you can speak to the moon? Perhaps she will have answer to what we are in the fix of things, do you suppose little Ivy you can speak to the moon? You are alive. We are dead things without a voice; perhaps the moon will hear you call her." "I certainly will call her, if she talks to the sea, she will talk to me." The sea rushed by and heard this, "Do not think she will talk to you I have tried for a billion years to get her to talk to me as to what purpose all this is, I have never gotten an answer." With that he swooshed by once again, making several cresting waves in frustration. "So then", said the Ivy, "when she rises tonight I will call on her. She cannot be so remote as not to hear my quest." "I wouldn't count on it, she never speaks to anyone." said the island "She is too far away hear a little ivy plant." "And she is far too concerned with her beauty." harumphed the pillar. "She has so many faces, you never know which one you are seeing, and, on top of that, talking to her, well no one ever talks to her, except, as I remember, lovers when she is full faced. She fairly drives humans mad when she is like that which is interesting, because she doesn't do a thing for me at any time." "But, what if I try anyway?" "Why not" said the island "You got the great sea to speak, why not the moon?"

That night the little Ivy plant drew up all its courage and when the moon rose looked at her and asked "great moon, will you speak with me?" The moon continued to rise and heard nothing.

The Ivy asked again, and the moon kept rising in the sky oblivious to anything that was happening on earth. She was her own sphere, and in her world, it seemed. Not the pillar or the ivy knew there was anything beyond them in their world. The island knew there was more, it had once been part of 'more', so had the pillar but pillar was a small part of that time. Now they lived in their own little universe. Each understood, in his way, this was not all there was. Each had a different idea of what 'more' meant.

The island knew that more meant; more land somewhere he was part of it, even though he was not connected to it.   The pillar knew what more meant to him; he had been part of a great edifice that had stood proud and important.   The fact he was alone didn't mean he hadn't been great, in his day. And the ivy knew what more meant to him. It meant there were other ivy plants somewhere, that he wasn't alone. The island, the pillar and the ivy knew they were not alone just because they were.   The great sea knew he wasn't alone because his waters mixed with other seas and in that he found he was part of something.

Every night when the moon rose, regardless her shape, the ivy would ask to speak to her, and every night the moon rose and set without saying anything.   The island went back to the business of musing about growth. The pillar stayed the course being tall and there, ever stalwart.   The ivy paused and wondered what it could do to make the moon respond, it could find nothing to make it work.

The little ivy plant sighed and went back to growing on the island. As time went on it grew. The island reclaimed some of its land from the sea, and the pillar stood against time, reluctantly permitting the ivy to grow up its column. Its reluctance was somewhat grudging because it felt it was not proper to have something growing on it, after all it, the pillar was a carved and ornate monument to the past. It hadn't thought it had some of its design eroded by time and weather, it remembered the past as it was and he was magnificent. The three spoke rarely.   It was one of those situations where proximity bred presence, and there was no need to talk.

One day the ivy sighed, its many leaves creating a hum as it rustled its noise. The island woke from a reverie, startled, and asked; "What was that?" "It wasn't me" said the pillar, "I've had nothing to say for a very long time." "It was me" said the ivy, "I have been wondering if I asked the moon once again to talk to me, if she would."
"Probably not", said the pillar, "As the great sea once told you; the moon speaks to no one, ever!"   "She just changes her moods and faces and runs the sea ragged" said the island, "She has no concern for what is here where we are.   She is much bigger than we are, so

why should she care what we think, or want?" "I don't know, but why shouldn't she care about us?" "Because she cares only about herself" roared the great sea, as he swooshed on cresting great waves in frustration.

The ivy was not daunted by all this; shy, perhaps, having been lectured by so many of his betters. 'But' he thought, "perhaps I can wake the moon if I sing to her." That day he practiced his song.

Then as the moon rose, at this time it was nearly full, the little ivy plant began to sing to the moon. He didn't have a voice as you and I know a 'voice', but he did have a very soft rustle which rose sweetly into the air. The island paid attention, and thought how sweet the noise was. The pillar heard the song and listened to the ivy sing. He was very impressed and wondered to himself what he would do if some one sang to him so sweetly. The great sea paused and lent his ear, he wanted to sing too so the moon would be sure to hear him if she were listening. The great sea began to sing. The song spread over the great sea to other shores where the tune was carried forth from there.

The moon continued her rise until she shown bright over all the sky. Her brightness dimmed the stars except for the brightest. From her place in the sky, she listened to the murmur in delight. It was not a noise she had ever heard before. True, she had heard much from the earth but always a noise she could ignore, most of it was flattery about her beauty, or being accused of making people mad in all ways; in love, in insanity, and other earthly demons. But this noise was a different sort and came from the little sea and then as she listened from the smallest of the small, an ivy plant. She was charmed, and she spoke, "Your song is very beautiful, I do not understand the words, will you tell me them?"

Well, no need to say the island and the pillar not to mention the great sea were all very much agog. The moon had never spoken to any one they knew of, it was very exciting. They waited for the ivy to collect himself wondering what he would say to the moon.

"Oh great moon, goddess of many faces, I would ask you a question, maybe two", said the ivy. "What question or two would you ask?" said the moon. "What do you see from your perch in the sky?" "Why, I see the earth as it turns every day", said the moon. "What is the earth?" asked the ivy. "Why it is the place you live, of course." "Is it very large?" "It is very large to you, but as you look at the sun, and the sun looks at the other stars, and the other stars look at the universe, we are all very small. I am tiny compared to all that, the sea you live in is tinier than me. Where you live is tiny to the sea." "Then we are nothing?" "No, you are not 'nothing', you are very small, even the smallest of us all is important to all his surroundings. In all the worlds there are, nothing is unimportant to its place and in its time. You and even I will one day become something else. When you die, your seeds will live and you will make them grow with your death. The island you live on will grow because you have taken root there so soil can stay on your shore and in time build a place for others to live." "Great moon how do you know all this?" "I have been here for millions of years and watched the earth change its land many times. I have seen everything come and go in their time, and all things die and in death bring new life to earth. The sun is the master of all we are, and it is he that gives me light. It is he that gives you light and dark, and warmth. If there were no sun, you could not live, and I could not shine as I do. It would all be darkness; even the great seas would be without life."

The pillar, ever vain asked, "Am I any thing in all this?" The moon laughed graciously, "Of course you are, but you too in time will see the end of it as will I. Nothing is forever, except forever" with that she sighed and asked, "sing your sweet tune again; it is time I slept for awhile. Remember I will always see you and how you sang to the moon, and made me very happy." The ivy, with the sea and the island and the pillar too, began to sing the song as a lullaby. As they did, the moon closed her eyes and slid below the horizon. They looked and saw the dawn begin to rise, as it always had, and they knew they were not alone, but part of a continuing cycle of existence which included everything, even them.

THE END

Acknowledgements:

THANK YOU

Linda Butta for all the work making the book wonderful!

Frank Boros for the illustrious illustrations.

Maritza Mcmillan for your grand graphic design and layout.

Jim Powers for your erudite editing.

Frank J. Boros
Visual Artist

My work begins with a scribble; the first impulse to put pencil to paper.   This inspiration, this need to get something down on paper has been my life from a very early age.

I received a Masters of Fine Arts degree from Yale University, for set and costume design in l969. Then I moved to New York City, where I, for over twenty years designed for Broadway, Off Broadway, Film, TV, The Calgary World's Fair, The Olympics and other venues.

In l990, I recreated myself as an artist, by closing my design studio and moving to Philadelphia to attend the Pennsylvania Academy of the Fine Arts.

Returning to New York City in 1994, I now live and work on the West Side of Manhattan, and travel a great deal. Various bodies of my work are inspired by my travels.   My most recent adventure was to Bhutan.